D0839432

Towards a Global Village

Institute for Policy Studies

The *Institute for Policy Studies* (IPS) is the United States' leading progressive think tank. Founded in 1963 by Richard Barnet and Marcus Raskin, IPS has remained in the forefront of research, advocacy, and experimentation on a variety of political, economic, and social issues. While the Fellows at the Institute do not embrace any one school of thought or 'ism', they are all working toward the goals of social reconstruction, economic justice, full employment, ecological sustainability, democratic participation, community empowerment, and demilitarization.

IPS Fellows and Research Fellows use four different strategies to promote their policy ideas: They influence opinion leaders by publishing books and articles in mainstream journals, magazines, and newspapers. They work closely with grassroots movements and provide them with useful information and analysis. They share with national, state, and local politicians critiques of current policies and designs of progressive alternatives. And they help create transnational networks of progressive public scholars, activists, and politicians.

Towns and Development

Towns and Development is a global network of NGOs (associations of local authorities, municipalities and community groups) working together to promote joint local action for North–South cooperation and sustainable development. This in the recognition that the only basis for real change and development lies in people themselves at local level. The Towns and Development network is associated with the International Union of Local Authorities (IULA).

After having supported conferences on joint local action in Europe, Africa and India, *Towns and Development* brought together more than 300 local authority and NGO representatives from 53 different countries in Berlin at the international North South Conference 'Local Initiatives for Sustainable Development'. The conference adopted the Berlin Charter and Action Agenda which has been translated into fourteen different languages and has been distributed and promoted worldwide.

The Berlin Charter sets out the wider 'political' framework for local initiatives. The Action Agenda is a summary of more than 100 action points formulated by the conference participants. Taken together, these documents outline the course that needs to be followed in the coming years.

The work of *Towns and Development* is based upon these documents and it pursues its aims through concrete action in public awareness raising and decentralised cooperation and by providing services to its members and other interested parties.

HN
49
C6
S52
1994

Towards a Global Village

International Community Development Initiatives

AAV4898

MICHAEL SHUMAN

Pluto  Press

LONDON • BOULDER, COLORADO

in association with

Towards and Development Institute for Policy Studies

First published 1994 by Pluto Press
345 Archway Road, London N6 5AA
in association with the Institute for Policy Studies, 1601 Connecticut Avenue
NW, Washington, DC 20009, USA and with Towns and Development, PO
Box 85615, 2508 CH The Hague, Netherlands

Copyright © Michael Shuman 1994

The right of Michael Shuman to be identified as the author of this work has
been asserted by him in accordance with sections 77 and 78 of the Copyright,
Designs and Patents Act 1988

British Library Cataloguing in Publication Data
A catalogue record for this book is available from the British Library

ISBN 0 7453 0861 9

Library of Congress Cataloging-in-Publication Data
Shuman, Michael.
  Towards a global village: international community development
initiatives / Michael Shuman.
  171p.   23cm.
  Includes bibliographical references and index.
  ISBN 0-7453-0861-9
  1. Community development. 2. International relations. 3. Cities
and towns. 4. Technical assistance. I. Title.
HN49.C6S52 1994
307.1'4–dc20   94–1728
                                                          CIP

Produced for the publishers by
Chase Production Services, Chipping Norton, UK
Typeset from author's disks by Stanford DTP Services, Milton Keynes, UK

Printed in Finland by WSOY

Contents

In memory of Musa Njue Njiru, a colleague and friend

Acknowledgments

The appearance of my name as author of this book is little more than a formality. The real credit goes to the tens of thousands of people worldwide who have involved their communities in North–South development cooperation. Among the most important of these organizers are the leaders of Towns and Development, a consortium of non-governmental organizations, local government associations, and community groups based in the Hague that has been promoting decentralized solutions to global problems since 1985.

This book originated in 1991, when Towns and Development was planning a conference in Berlin to evaluate half a decade of work. Thirty-eight papers were commissioned from 21 countries and a dozen "issue networks" to understand what appeared to be an emerging movement of globally conscientious and active communities. My assignment was to integrate these papers into a short, readable conference report. After the conference the board of Towns and Development decided that this report should be rewritten, updated, expanded, and distributed to a larger audience in the form of this book.

There are many people who helped make completion of this book possible. I would like to thank, first, the authors of the country reports who provided most of the research and factual input for the book: Eduardo Galeazzi and Juan Luis Merega (Argentina), Brigid Weinzinger and Franz Schmidjell (Austria), Jan Demedts (Belgium), Juan Vergara (Chile), Mikko Lohikoski (Finland), Norbert Noisser (Germany), Pantelis Sklias (Greece), Manohar Golpelwar (India), Gioia Maestro (Italy), Shin Yoshida (Japan), Mathew Kibe (Kenya), Paul van Tongeren (Netherlands), Monica Baltodano (Nicaragua), Tor Henrik Andersen (Norway), Horacio Morales Jr. (Philippines), Clara Delia Caballero Caraballo (Spain), Jane Knight and Mary Sheaff (United Kingdom), Gabriel Banda (Zambia), and Gladys Maseko (Zimbabwe). With the brilliant research assistance of Ona Alston, I was able to prepare country reports on the United States and Canada.

Equally important inputs to the Berlin conference report were provided by the authors of papers on networks of cities involved in various issues: Hans Buis (anti-apartheid initiatives), Anne Yarwood (development education, a Northern perspective), Moussa Conteh (development education, a Southern perspective), Ron Kingham and Simon Petten (environmental protection, a Northern perspective), Renu Wadehra (environmental protection, a Southern perspective), Arjan Agema (human rights), Ronald van der Hijden (Nicaragua linking),

Manab Chakraborty (North–South economic relations), Ben ter Veer (peace activities and East–West relations), Alf Dubbs and Alex Neve (refugees), Udo Sprang (solidarity coffee), Seydou Sall (South–South relations), Erik-Jan Hertogs (technical assistance), Jane Knight (twinning, a Northern perspective), Peter Nyoni (twinning, a Southern perspective), and Dion van den Berg (Yugoslavian peace initiatives).

Early drafts of the conference report went through extensive peer review at a series of meetings at Kontakt der Kontinenten in Soesterberg, Netherlands. Among the commenters who made my life considerably more difficult—but the product considerably better—were Markus Adelsbach, Peter Batty, Dion van den Berg, Paul Bongers, Manohar Golpelwar, Nelke van Heest, Erik-Jan Hertogs, Gunther Hilliges, Jane Knight, Jos Lemmers, Godfrey Nhemachena, Jacob Noe, Jan Rademaker, Peter Slits, Heikki Telakivi, Jürgen Varnhorn, Renu Wadehra, and Frances Weijn. Another person who offered gentle, constructive criticism throughout these meetings was Musa Njiru, who tragically died in a fire in Lisbon while helping us prepare for the conference and to whom I have dedicated this book.

I owe special thanks to Paul van Tongeren, currently the chair of Towns and Development. Paul's friends say that every hour with him generates a week of work, but my experience suggests that this is an underestimate. I am indebted to Paul for involving me in Towns and Development, for providing room and board at critical moments, for lobbying his reluctant colleagues to support the preparation of a conference report and this book, and for making sure that every unused hour of my time was consumed with community-based development initiatives.

In the process of transforming the conference report into a book, I also was privileged to receive useful comments from two of the best thinkers on alternative strategies for development: Susan George and David Korten.

My biggest thanks goes to the heroes of this book—the citizens, activists, churchgoers, businessmen, city councilors, and countless others who are seeking to create a better world through local initiatives. Ignoring the cynical pronouncements of mainstream politicians, *Realpolitik* political scientists, and neoclassical economists, that only national elite can influence international affairs, these local leaders are making their own history and demonstrating that one of the most important and unappreciated strategies to achieve world peace, justice, and sustainability is to create a powerful global network of communities. My hope, shared by my colleagues at Towns and Development, is that you will be inspired by the stories in the following pages to mobilize your own community to become part of the global village.

Michael H. Shuman
December 1993

The sudden changes in Eastern Europe, the vanishing borders between East and West, changed our picture of the world. Do we not actually live within one single world, a global village? The world as one society, a village that has a countless number of slums. Slums that are filled with street urchins, people that have no homes, no schools, no education, no health care, no idea as to where tomorrow's earnings will come from, no work...The world is rapidly changing and we can no longer afford to turn our backs on it. The problems we are facing are worldwide. In fact, there is not one single country left that can make its own decisions. We have slowly become part of a world community, a world market, a world economy. This awareness should be passed on to our fellow citizens, and especially in this area—I repeat this—this is an important responsibility for municipalities.

— Dr Jan P. Pronk, Dutch Minister for Development Cooperation

Introduction

Global Communities

As the world moves into the twenty-first century, it enters a period of unprecedented crisis and opportunity. Faced with global warming, ozone depletion, and
nuclear proliferation, the human race can no longer take the future for granted.
Millions of people have decided to try to solve the planet's problems through
local action. In thousands of cities, towns, and villages, community groups and
non-governmental organizations (NGOs) are teaming up with local authorities
to remold international relations, particularly relations between the wealthy
countries of the North and the poor countries of the South. Here is a small sampling
of what has occurred over the past decade:

- Nearly two thousand Northern communities have links with communities
  in the South, and many of these ties have led to working relationships between
  schools, hospitals, universities, fire departments, environmental groups,
  unions, and municipal governments.
- A number of countries in the European Community make development
  education a standard feature of the curriculum of primary and secondary
  schools, and several – including Denmark, Germany, Netherlands, and the
  United Kingdom – have set up a network of local development education
  centers which provide materials, information, and training to the general
  public.
- The city-state of Bremen in Germany, with a population of 750,000, gives
  about DM 1 million ($608,600) in grants per year to NGOs and community
  groups active on North–South issues.
- When Dushanbe, a city in the former Soviet Union, faced a serious food
  shortage in 1990, its sister city of Lusaka in Zambia rushed in emergency
  shipments of fruits and vegetables.
- Sixty communities in the Netherlands are now helping counterparts in the
  South and East to cope with environmental and administrative problems
  by sending Dutch civil servants to be on–site advisors and by training
  Southern and Eastern town officers.
- In the United States 27 states, 25 counties, and 101 cities enacted anti-
  apartheid sanctions, causing 200 out of the 300 US companies doing

1

business in South Africa to leave or sell off their equity interests, and forcing the US government to drop its policy of "constructive engagement."

• After Amadeo Lopez, mayor of San Antonio Los Ranchos, was imprisoned and tortured by the 4th brigade of the Salvadoran armed forces, the mayor and city council of Berkeley, California, successfully lobbied US and Salvadoran officials to release the official without harm.

These local initiatives, most of which began in the 1980s, rarely grab national headlines. Indeed, most communities are only dimly aware of the international work being done in their own country, let alone by communities in distant parts of the world. This book represents the first comprehensive effort to define, track, and analyze this emerging global movement of community-based development initiatives. Its aim is to lift these initiatives from obscurity and place them into the mainstream of global affairs.

What are CDIs?

The term *community-based development initiatives*, or CDIs, refers to actions undertaken jointly by NGOs, community groups, and local governments to promote global development. CDIs, at least as used here, do not include development initiatives undertaken exclusively by NGOs or citizens' groups. Nor do they include purely local initiatives to boost a city's economy or to clean up its environment (unless these initiatives relate to larger international issues). Instead, they refer to policies that reach beyond the borders of a community.

The term *development*, according to the Brundtland Commission, means "meeting the basic needs of all and extending to all the opportunity to fulfil their aspirations for a better life." By this definition, development encompasses more than just increasing the income level of people living in poor countries; it also requires improving the requisites of "a better life" – equity, human rights, democracy, environmental protection, and peace. This broad conception of development grows out of the failures of earlier development efforts, when Northerners imposed inappropriate economic models throughout the South. The costs of these earlier mistakes are now well known: a $1.4 trillion debt that countries of the South may never be able to repay; "structural adjustment" programs that increased poverty, unemployment, and suffering throughout the South; and trade-based economies that are destroying communities, families, and the environment virtually everywhere.

The practitioners of CDIs are interested in what they call people-centered development. They are less concerned with the traditional indices of wealth than with the essentials for a high quality of life, such as literacy, technological know-how, self-reliance, healthy ecosystems, demilitarization, and – most importantly – personal empowerment. They believe that only a small part of the "problem of development" is the provision of aid, loans, investment, and technology to the South. Equally important, and urgent, is to change the economic, environmental, and military policies of the North.

Once development is defined in people-centered terms, the importance of communities comes sharply into focus. Communities are the institutions for political action that are closest to the people. Communities in the South are much more capable than their national governments of understanding the needs of their people and of designing constructive policies. Communities in the North can mobilize citizens for political action faster and more decisively than their national governments can. Together, Southern and Northern communities can work together through people-to-people relationships that are non-bureaucratic and motivating.

Communities can use any legal power they possess to promote people-centered development. Most CDIs fall into ten categories:

Education. Many communities raise public awareness on development issues through schools, campaigns, pen-pal relationships, Third World fairs, exhibitions, debates, and films.

Linking and Twinning. Some Northern and Southern cities formally adopt one another, opening up relations between all types of groups within their jurisdictions: youth organizations, doctors, lawyers, teachers, taxi drivers, police, firefighters, and housewives.

Project Support. Many Northern communities sponsor or finance development efforts in the South that range from building sewage treatment facilities to installing biogas digesters.

Technical and Administrative Assistance. Civil servants running local governments in the North are increasingly assisting their counterparts in the South through training and collaboration.

Campaigning. Communities can lobby national leaders, parliamentarians, and bureaucrats – both their own and others' – to change policies concerning trade, deforestation, human rights abuses, or hundreds of other global issues of concern.

Preferences and Sanctions. Communities can put pressure on corporations and politicians by carefully investing their money in and entering into contracts with companies that are behaving well in North–South relations.

Regulation. Similarly, communities can force multinational corporations to change their international behavior by regulating the way they do business locally.

Institutions. Many communities professionalize their CDIs by creating what are effectively local departments of development cooperation.

International Agreements. Groups of communities are also promoting CDIs through special global pacts and organizations.

Grants. Finally, communities are giving away tens of millions of dollars in grants of money to grassroots promoters of CDIs at home and abroad.

What Have CDIs Accomplished?

Communities have used CDI tools to influence almost every conceivable issue in people-centered development. Their biggest successes have been scored in protecting the earth's environment, promoting human rights, mobilizing international opposition to the Nicaraguan contras, weakening apartheid, and improving East–West relations.

Communities moved much faster than their national governments in the fight against global warming, ozone depletion, and deforestation. They initiated comprehensive programs to conserve energy and water, to build bicycle paths and mass transit, to plant trees, to ban chlorofluorocarbons, to recycle wastes, and to avoid using tropical timber. Over 150 European municipalities joined the Climate Alliance, committing themselves to cutting carbon-dioxide emissions in half by the year 2010. The Green Campaign in Colombia pushed the nation's thousand-plus municipalities to rethink their development plans in more environmentally sensitive ways. The International Council for Local Environmental Initiatives (ICLEI) now helps several hundred municipalities worldwide share state-of-the-art technologies and policies for environmental protection.

Communities have also taken up human rights causes ignored or overlooked by their governments. At least one hundred US mayors have worked with Amnesty International in adopting prisoners of conscience. Mayor Larry Agran of Irvine, California, flew to Vietnam to plead for the release of 30 political prisoners. In the mid-1970s several Dutch cities threatened to cut off their municipal contracts with Stevin, a major dredging and building firm, unless it canceled its projects for the repressive regime of General Augusto Pinochet in Chile. To protect human rights in their own backyards, local governments throughout Western Europe are struggling to treat refugees from the East and South with basic standards of decency.

Perhaps the most dramatic example of the potential of CDIs is the global campaign against apartheid. Hundreds of cities in Europe and the United States divested tens of billions of dollars from firms doing business in South Africa, and many canceled municipal contracts with these firms. This movement was responsible for Northern corporations leaving South Africa en masse, Northern governments implementing sanctions, and the regime in Pretoria beginning to undertake internal reforms. Supplementing these pressure groups were sister-community relationships that assisted black civic associations in South Africa.

Another success story occurred in Nicaragua, where about three hundred US and European cities established solidarity links. Besides providing substantial levels of aid (in many Nicaraguan towns, donations from Northern cities made up over half of their capital budgets), these linkings mobilized international pressure against the US-sponsored contra war. The 86 US-Nicaraguan sister cities sent more humanitarian assistance to Nicaraguan towns than all the aid the US government provided to the contras, and managed to keep US public opinion two-to-one against contra aid (ultimately, Congress pulled the plug on President Reagan's contra program in 1988).

Finally, municipalities played a key role in defusing the Cold War in Europe. By declaring themselves "nuclear free," enacting public education programs to reverse the arms race, and linking with cities in the Soviet Union and Eastern Europe, hundreds of communities in the West were able to remold East–West relations. Once characterized by cultural exchanges and good-will visits, these ties now emphasize economic cooperation and the building of civil society. In 1991, for example, the Dutch provided training for 150 officials and civil servants from Poland, Hungary, and Czechoslovakia.

How Have CDIs Evolved?

Four recent developments can explain the rise of CDIs. First, the growing impact of global problems such as acid rain and immigration at the local level forces responsible municipal decision-makers to make solving these problems a integral part of their jobs. Second, the declining costs of global transportation and communication give every community the means to engage in some form of international politicking. This has been accelerated, third, by the spread of democracy in the East and South (however falteringly), which has given hundreds of millions of citizens who were once silenced the freedom to speak out, to travel, and to participate in international affairs. A fourth trend is the renewed importance of community, which provides people with a new platform on which to organize themselves politically. These factors suggest why CDIs have emerged in countries on every continent (except Antarctica).

Of course, CDIs have developed faster in some countries than in others. Belgium, the Netherlands, and the United Kingdom built their CDIs on economic and cultural ties to their old colonies and a principal motivation was a sense of responsibility about past acts of exploitation. In the United States, African Americans orchestrated the sanctions movement against South Africa and Hispanic Americans pressed for solidarity ties with Nicaragua and El Salvador. Other factors contributing to one community's interest in another include language affinities, similar city names, and dynamic individual organizers.

Critics of CDIs sometimes claim that communities are "meddling" in international affairs and that foreign policy should be exclusively under the authority of national officials. But there are at least six reasons why a growing number of local governments believe that international affairs are their affairs. CDIs provide people with practical means to recognize, and to be recognized by, others thousands of miles away. They enable citizens to act on their feelings of global responsibility and rectify global inequities. They provide accessible tools for people to fix global problems such as wars, ozone depletion, or the illegal drug trade, and they help communities strengthen the powers of local governance worldwide. They enable communities to enjoy economic benefits through aid, loans, technology transfer, or trade. They enrich community life by drawing in foreign cultures and by promoting habits of tolerance, understanding, and empathy for foreigners. And they enhance political participation by building bridges of cooperation between citizens and local political institutions.

For all these reasons, CDIs have sprung up spontaneously throughout the world. But in the 1970s and 1980s, the spread of CDIs was accelerated through the concerted work of individuals, NGOs, community groups, local governments, and national agencies. Among the key leaders were Oxfam in the United Kingdom, the city-state of Bremen in Germany, and the National Ministry of Development Education in the Netherlands. Most national governments initially treated CDIs with indifference or hostility, but over time they sought to cooperate with enterprising cities.

Bolstering efforts to promote CDIs within various nations has been an international organization called "Towns and Development." A conference held in 1983 in Florence, Italy, co-sponsored by the United Towns Organisation (UTO), the International Union of Local Authorities (IULA), and the United Nations Educational, Scientific, and Cultural Organization (UNESCO), revealed that a surprisingly large number of municipalities in Western Europe were involved in North–South issues. Because very few NGOs and community groups participated in the Florence Conference, Gunther Hilliges from Bremen and Paul van Tongeren from Amsterdam organized another conference two years later in Cologne, West Germany. This time official and unofficial actors were represented equally. Leaders from 130 organizations and from communities in twelve countries attended and issued a two-page "appeal" calling for a fundamentally new approach to North–South cooperation.

Subtitled "From Charity to Justice," the Cologne Appeal called for local authorities, NGOs, and community groups to undertake joint action to supplement national and international development efforts. The document contained several striking points:

- "While aid is welcome and necessary for those who suffer from injustice, aid is insufficient for achieving a genuine solution."
- "The interrelations of the problems of environment, development and disarmament must be taken into account in any analysis of the North–South partnership."
- As important as economic assistance is for the South, it is even more imperative "to recognize the need for structural change in the international economic and social order with implications for our own societies."
- Decentralization of North–South work is "the starting-point for raising public awareness leading to a more comprehensive understanding of North–South problems (including the problems in the North)."

- Community-based development projects should emphasize "equality, reciprocity, [and the] absence of paternalism;" proceed with the full "initiation and approval of projects by the partner communities;" "focus on the poorest in developing countries and the poorest countries;" recognize "the significance of women in development;" "take account of the environmental impact of projects in advance;" and "maintain cultural diversity."

The drafters of the Cologne Appeal set up Towns and Development to begin translating and distributing the document throughout Europe. With financial support from the European Commission, the organization helped mobilize more than a thousand European localities to launch one kind of CDI or another. Periodic meetings, publications, and conferences widened the organization's steering committee to include representatives from Austria, Belgium, Finland, Germany, Greece, Italy, Netherlands, Norway, Spain, and the United Kingdom, as well as from IULA, UTO, and the London-based Local Government International Bureau. Informal relationships were established with CDI practitioners in Japan, Norway, Portugal, and the United States.

In 1990 Towns and Development joined up with the United Kingdom One World Linking Association (UKOWLA) and with a group of African NGOs, community groups, and local authorities to hold a conference in Bulawayo, Zimbabwe, entitled "South–North Linking for Development." This was the first time that NGO leaders, civil servants, and local officials from the South came together to discuss their own views of CDIs. It was also one of the few conferences to consider linking as a tool not only for people-to-people exchange but also for sustainable development. Buoyed by the enthusiastic response in Africa, Indian NGOs and local authorities organized a similar conference in Sevagram, where 126 delegates issued an appeal for joint action for sustainable development in India.

Where is the CDI Movement Heading?

In October 1992, Towns and Development held a conference in Berlin to assess the progress CDIs have made since the meetings in Florence and Cologne. Organized in cooperation with the North–South Centre of the Council of Europe, and supported by, among others, the German government and the State of Berlin, the conference attracted 300 representatives from 52 countries. The conveners commissioned 38 "input papers" from the leading theorists and practitioners on CDIs from around the world. Twenty-two of these papers charted the progress of CDIs in specific countries (14 in the North and eight in the South). The other papers, so-called "issue reports," described global networks that had formed either around specific types of CDIs (development education, twinning and linking, technical cooperation) or around specific issues (environmental protection, apartheid, Nicaraguan solidarity, human rights, East–West relations, South–South relations).

These papers and subsequent discussions revealed numerous problems within the CDI movement. The following were among the most salient:

- Very little is known about CDIs in most countries.
- Serious evaluation by either Southern or Northern partners is practically non-existent.
- Development educators are often content to spread information rather than to stimulate critical thinking or to imbue citizens with a sense of personal responsibility that can lead to political action.
- CDI practitioners have not done enough to protect the global environment by changing the lifestyles of the rich in both the North and South.
- Most CDIs fail to address the two most fundamental issues concerning North–South economic relations: the $1.4 trillion debt the South owes to the North, and the unfair structure of world trade.
- Northern and Southern partners too often embrace the precepts of free trade rather than promote self-reliance and "alternative trade" relations among their poorest citizens.
- Northerners have not done enough to help their Southern partners establish new, empowering relations with other communities in the South.
- Too many communities are politically timid about shaping CDIs to address human rights abuses, refugee problems, and wars – all crucial issues for people-centered development.
- CDI practitioners in the North continue to focus disproportionate time and effort on raising money to aid the South.
- Many CDI relationships are characterized by paternalism and imbalance, with Northerners not learning as much as Southerners.
- Some East–West links are now displacing North–South links rather than strengthening them.
- CDI promoters are doing little to strengthen the powers and rights of local governments at home and abroad.
- Too many communities are failing to create institutions responsible for CDIs within their local government that are staffed by civil servants and supported by municipal funds.
- Many communities with CDIs are finding that close working relations with national ministries constitute a devil's bargain, where the benefits of national financial assistance may be outweighed by the costs of losing independence.

The participants in the Berlin Conference responded to these challenges with two documents, a charter and an action plan, both of which contained extensive recommendations for local governments, NGOs, and community groups. Like the Cologne Appeal, these short pieces are now being distributed throughout Europe by Towns and Development. Thus far they have been translated into

Dutch, Finnish, French, German, Greek, Hindi, Italian, Japanese, Maharati, Norwegian, Portuguese, Spanish, and Swedish.

As the Berlin Charter and Action Plan are spread around the world, the movement will continue to grow. Just how powerful it ultimately will become remains to be seen. If the criticisms of initiatives undertaken thus far are ignored, CDIs could become trivial at best or, at worst, replicate the disastrous mistakes of national development policies. But if the movement follows the recommendations articulated in Berlin, it has a chance – just a chance – to change the face of history.

Organization of the Book

This book is divided into six chapters. Chapter 1 describes the context for community-based development initiatives: the failure of existing models of development; the advantages of an alternative approach that is people-centered, multidimensional, and two-way; and the ways in which communities can promote this alternative. Chapter 2 lays out ten different types of CDI tools. Chapter 3 shows how communities have used these tools to protect the global environment, to promote human rights, to weaken apartheid, to end the civil war in Nicaragua, to strengthen East–West relations, and to support South–South relations. Chapter 4 examines the global, national, and local reasons why these initiatives are occurring. Chapter 5 looks at how five different players in international affairs have responded to community activism: NGOs and community groups, local authorities, national governments, international organizations, and women. Chapter 6 critically evaluates community-based development initiatives by reviewing the challenges the movement now faces.

To help readers start their own CDIs, the book concludes with three appendices. Appendix I contains short summaries of the CDI movement in 22 countries. Appendix II has the leading statements of the movement from Cologne, Bulawayo, Sevagram, and Berlin. And Appendix III presents lists of key contact people, publications, and other resources.

CHAPTER 1

Context

The terms North and South, as introduced in 1980 by the report of the Brandt Commission, *North-South: A Programme for Survival*, and subsequently used by development practitioners, were and are misleading. As a matter of pure geography some countries north of the equator are relatively poor (such as India and Pakistan), while others to the south are relatively rich (such as Australia and New Zealand). Moreover, every country in the North has people who live in poverty, and every country in the South has people who are wealthy, even by Northern standards. And there is an increasing geographical scrambling of North and South as an estimated 75 million Southerners leave their homes each year, traveling North to find jobs or to escape from war and repression. Nevertheless, the terms North and South capture an essential reality of our time: the enormous gap between rich and poor in an increasingly interdependent world.

There is a growing recognition that the fate of the North is inextricably linked to the fate of the South. The Brandt Commission pointed out that the economically developed North could no longer take the 3.4 billion people living in the South (now 4 billion) for granted. Without the South's resources, workers, and markets, the North would face certain economic decline. "Development" was no longer an act of charity; it was necessary for the North's economic survival.

The 1987 report of the Brundtland Commission, *Our Common Future*, further highlighted the interdependence of North and South. It concluded that Northern overconsumption and Southern poverty were destroying the planet's precious ecological life-support systems. Noting emerging disasters such as ozone depletion and global warming, the commission urged that development proceed on an environmentally sound and sustainable basis. The term "sustainable development" has since become the talisman of thousands of conferences, declarations, and position papers.

But thus far development and sustainable development have remained distant, unfulfilled goals. To be sure, Northern initiatives have pumped up the statistics for gross national product, literacy, and life expectancy in many Southern nations. But the overall legacy of the North's economic relations with the South has been $1.4 trillion of debt, worsening terms of trade, and harsh austerity programs imposed by the International Monetary Fund (IMF) and other multilateral banks. Indeed, the level of official development aid has actually declined over the past decade, and more financial resources are now flowing *from* the nations of the South than *to* them (more than $50 billion net in 1989). Moreover, many large-scale development projects in the South promoted by the World Bank and other lending authorities have come under attack for unleashing environmental havoc, social upheaval, and increased poverty. Noting the burdens which AIDs, population growth, and ecological degradation will add in the 1990s, a recent World Bank report foresees a "growing trend of increasing impoverishment."

This trend could worsen if, as many fear, the North simply abandons the South, now that the Cold War is over. Even though the need for North–South cooperation has never been greater, the limited results of the 1992 United Nations Conference on Environment and Development (UNCED) in Rio de Janeiro underscore that many nations are simply unwilling to change their behavior for the global good.

If national governments had figured out how to eradicate the injustices and environmental disasters facing the world, CDIs would be entirely unnecessary. But the history of development since World War Two has been one of disappointment and disillusionment. As the Washington-based Worldwatch Institute recently reported:

> Since 1950, the gap between rich and poor nations has grown mostly because the rich got richer. But since 1980, in many developing countries the poor have been getting poorer too. Forty-three developing nations probably finished the decade poorer, in per capita terms, than they started it.

The failure of conventional development has convinced a growing number of citizens and non-governmental organizations to redefine development in "people-centered" terms, which not only invites community action but demands it.

New Thinking on Development

Far removed from the IMF, the World Bank, and most national development agencies is a loose network of concerned citizens, non-governmental organizations (NGOs), and community groups interested in a fundamentally new approach to development. Most of these people barely know one another, let alone work together. But throughout the North, South, and East they have drawn remarkably similar conclusions: that development should be people-based, multidimensional, and two-way.

A People-centered Approach

There is an emerging consensus among grassroots groups, particularly the victims of the North's counterproductive development initiatives, that the traditional indices of progress – high GNP growth, a positive balance of trade, an appreciating currency, high levels of consumption – actually say very little about the quality of people's lives. The most important questions are, unfortunately, less susceptible to quantitative analysis: Are people, particularly poor people, gaining more power over their daily circumstances? Are their lives becoming more rewarding, more satisfying? Are their families and communities getting stronger? Are their cultures and ecosystems being conserved?

Tanzanian President Julius Nyerere once said:

> Development means the development of people. Roads, buildings, the increases of crop output, and other things of this nature are not development; they are only tools of development.... An increase in the number of school buildings is development only if those buildings can be, and are being, used to develop the minds and understanding of people. An increase in the output of wheat or maize, or beans, is only development if it leads to better nutrition of people. An expansion of cotton, coffee, or sisal crop is development only if these can be sold and the money used for other things which improve the health, comfort, and understanding of the people.

The most basic role of development policy should be to empower people to gain control over their own destiny, especially the poorest of the poor, who have the least political power. As Nyerere has suggested:

> [P]eople cannot be developed; they can only develop themselves. For while it is possible for an outsider to build a man's house, an outsider cannot give the man the pride and self-confidence in himself as a human being. Those things a man has to create in himself by his own actions. He develops himself by what he does; he develops himself by making his own decisions, by increasing his understanding of what he is doing and why, by increasing his own knowledge and ability, and his own full participation – as an equal – in the life of the community he lives in.

Of course, Nyerere's observation applies with equal force to women.

But self-empowerment is not enough. A people-centered approach requires respect for others: respect for one's family, one's neighbors, one's community, one's environment, one's culture, and one's world. This can be done only by embracing a larger agenda than "economic progress."

Development as a Multidimensional Agenda

If the goal of development is to empower and heighten respect, and not just to pump up abstract economic indicators, many goals once deemed peripheral become central. Consequently, people-centered development encompasses a broad agenda that includes participation, environmental sustainability, equity, and demilitarization.

Participation is the first requisite for development. Without the freedom to speak, assemble, publish, or travel, people cannot become masters of their own destiny. Nor can they do so if their economic rights to food, shelter, medical care, or housing are denied. These rights, all enshrined in the Universal Declaration of Human Rights, the Helsinki Final Act, and many other treaties, are necessary ingredients for personal empowerment.

Meaningful participation also requires that people have the freedom to choose their own leaders. Autocratic and totalitarian states are prone to wage war, to infringe on people's basic human rights, to stifle individual initiative, and to drain people's productivity. While democracy has had its longest history in the West, it is worth pointing out that political participation rates are falling in established democracies such as the United States and the United Kingdom. All countries, including those of the West, are in profound need of democratic reform.

A second requirement for development is environmental sustainability. Every community should live within its ecological carrying capacity to the greatest extent possible. It should try to maximize use of renewable resources and minimize consumption of depletable resources through recycling and simpler lifestyles. It should seek to eliminate releases of pollutants and toxics into the global environment. Whether communities ever can achieve self-sufficiency is unclear, but certainly they should *attempt* to move in this direction. The world no longer can afford to dismiss environmental destruction, as neoclassical economists have, as a regrettable "externality."

A third requirement for development is equity. Most economists gloss over questions of distribution, but who gains and who loses is central to whether or not human progress is really occurring. Development can disempower the majority if it enables a small number of people in a given country to control most of the wealth, to buy elections and television stations, to monopolize printing presses, and to control the voices of opinion leaders. Gross income disparities – both within nations and between them – invite slavery, peonage, and exploitation. Redistribution is necessary to give the weakest members of society a modicum of control over their future.

A final requirement for development is demilitarization. Even though the Cold War is over, the nations of the world continue to squander nearly a trillion dollars per year on armaments and war. If these resources are ever to be freed up for development, deep cuts in military spending will be necessary. Thus, arms control, United Nations peacekeeping, non-provocative defense, and conflict resolution, all of which can enable nations to cut military spending without reducing their security, are relevant to development.

Development is a Two-way Street

Traditionally, development was viewed as a process that the rich countries of the North "helped" poor countries of the South to do. In the name of alleviating "Third World misery," the North provided aid, loans, investments, and technology. This conception of development, however, was flawed in three respects.

First, as already noted, the net impact on the South of all the North's help was negative, as debt payments outswamped the value of assistance by the early 1980s. Indeed, even the use of terms such as "help" and "assistance" masked the inequitable nature of the economic relations between North and South.

Second, those on the receiving end bristled from the paternalism of well-intentioned Northerners who dared to tell Southerners how they should lead their lives. Musa Njiru of Kenya told the participants of a CDI conference in Bulawayo, Zimbabwe: "If the North really wants to help, it should be doing this by giving back to the people in the South their self-confidence, so this superiority/inferiority relationship can be brought to an end."

To overcome paternalism, the North must begin to see development as a way not just to instruct but to learn. Njiru reminded his audience in Bulawayo that even the aborigines of Australia and Yanomani Indians of the Amazon have much to teach the North:

> By our civilised standards and judgement these communities appear backward and primitive, with their lives bordering closely on savagery; but their lives as a group were more cohesive and stable, their education deceptively simple but appropriate and adequate, and above all they tended to live in harmony with the environment.

A third problem with the one-way model of development is that it deflects attention from ways in which the North is creating and exacerbating poverty in the South. Wasteful consumption by Northerners is the primary culprit for global warming and ozone depletion, two imminent environmental catastrophes that will have especially devastating impacts on the world's poor. Deficit spending by the United States has raised interest charges on the South's debts by many billions of dollars. Weapons shipments, covert actions, and armed interventions from the North have enabled dictators in the South to repress grassroots movements seeking land reform and economic justice. Corporations from the North have plundered oil, minerals, and forests that otherwise might have supported real development in the South.

A small but growing number of self-reflective Northerners are becoming aware of the shortcomings of the old, one-way model of development. They are beginning to recognize that relieving poverty in the South is impossible without fundamental change in the North. Unless Northerners change their profligate lifestyle, eliminate their national deficits, redirect their military spending toward economic justice in the South, renounce armed interventions, rein in their corporations, and change their paternalist attitudes, meaningful development will be extraordinarily difficult. A people-centered approach to development invites Northerners and Southerners to come to the table as equals, to recognize the interconnected nature of their problems, to seek political change in both regions. It is built on the assumption that people from any place have much to teach and much to learn. Northerners and Southerners can best work together if their relationships are characterized by balance and mutual respect.

Community-based Development Initiatives

One implication of a people-centered approach to development is the critical importance of local action. NGOs, community groups, and local authorities, when they work together, can promote people-centered development by empowering ordinary citizens to take action, by taking advantage of expertise at the local level, and by opening conduits for change outside of national bureaucracies.

CDIs Facilitate Empowerment

Community action helps development practitioners achieve the most salient goal of people-centered development – namely, empowerment. What empowers people varies enormously. Some individuals need education or housing, while others need land reform or new political institutions. Women may require better legal protection of their property rights. Refugees settling in a new homeland may need language instruction and short-term economic assistance. Any generalization is fraught with danger, and a policy that successfully empowers one person may be irrelevant or disempowering for another.

A fundamental limitation of the programs of the IMF, the World Bank, and most national development agencies is that they are based on an infatuation with macroeconomics; they lump people together, homogenize diverse needs, ignore special cases. They posit general prescriptions for an almost infinite variety of ills. Large-scale development programs also are hampered by multiple layers of bureaucracy on both the giving and receiving ends. A technocrat who never meets the people that his or her decisions affect is likely to be insensitive to their needs. The more layers of red tape that lie between provider and beneficiary of assistance, the greater the difficulty to communicate, to set a joint agenda, to make mid-course adjustments, and to take into account special needs.

By directly involving NGOs, community groups, and local authorities – the very institutions closest to people – CDIs are more likely than conventional development initiatives to meet the needs of the world's poor. As the Brundtland Commission noted: "NGOs and private and community groups can often provide an efficient and effective alternative to public agencies in the delivery of programmes and projects. Moreover, they can sometimes reach target groups that public agencies cannot."

The people-to-people relationships that characterize CDIs are often energizing, inspiring, and motivating. Personal contact, says one Norwegian involved in linking, "creates positive attitudes [about] development aid, because it gives us information about real needs and indicates how financial aid can best be applied." With the bonds of friendship, partners can jointly plan, implement, and evaluate a development project, and they can make modifications if an unexpected environmental or social problem turns up.

CDIs aim to create global change. Most national and international development agencies have a mandate to help the South, not to change the North. CDIs, in contrast, emphasize the need for changes in consciousness and behavior in both regions. According to another Norwegian linking participant: "Visits from abroad give new impulses and raise the level of awareness and understanding."

CDIs enable Northerners and Southerners to cut otherwise staggering international problems down to size. Working together, NGOs and local authorities can analyze how North–South relations affect the community, and how the community can constructively affect North–South relations. A Northern community might decide to become more sustainable, or it might decide to regulate the behavior of a local corporation with operations in the South. Unlike national action, which requires a slow process of building a nationwide consensus before any actions can go forward, community action can begin almost immediately. And once one CDI succeeds, a community is empowered to adopt others.

With CDIs, citizen organizations can press local authorities to act more effectively. As Gioia Maestro of Italy notes: "Where this pressure of the townspeople was stronger, due to cultural and social traditions, the activities of the local authority became significant; whereas where the pressure of the townspeople was weaker, the council became passive."

NGOs and community groups can identify special problems in international affairs and propose innovative solutions. But they often lack resources and legitimacy. That is where local governments can help. Even though local governments are not wealthy, their budgets are far larger than those of most NGOs or community groups. In Norway the involvement of local authorities in development work has given grassroots groups access to information distribution networks, to data-processing services, and to telecommunications technologies. The involvement of a mayor or the city council can give a CDI the imprimatur of respectability that may be necessary for the media to pay attention. And once the mayor, city council members, and civil servants are engaged in North–South issues, development cooperation acquires a momentum that is difficult to stop.

CDIs Harness Local Expertise

Community action also promotes people-centered development by transferring expertise from one locality to another. Being the level of government closest to the people, a local authority often knows a great deal about how to ensure that people are fed, educated, housed, and employed. Local authorities have principal responsibility for removing trash, preventing crime, fixing roads and street-lamps, extinguishing fires, coping with natural disasters, and fighting sexism and racism. No serious development effort aimed at, say, building a clean water system in San Salvador can proceed very far without involving that city's water engineers.

CDIs enable municipal experts from North and South to come together and learn from each other. The fire department of Amsterdam, for example, helped its counterpart in Beira, Mozambique, by sending two fire engines (with spare parts) and training the Beiran fire-fighters to operate and maintain the equipment.

The broad agenda of people-centered development also can benefit from local expertise. Demilitarization demands local planning to convert old missile factories and air bases into productive peacetime enterprises. Participation is possible only if local police protect the rights of citizens to speak, assemble, organize, travel, and publish. Environmental protection ultimately requires local implementation. And equity can be realized only if the poor receive equal protection under municipal law, if local taxes are progressive, and if communities take care of the basic needs of the poor. In each of these policy areas, Northern and Southern communities can learn from one another.

Many local government officials have one additional skill that is important to development: the ability to resolve conflicts without violence. Every day mayors and councilors are called upon to prevent street fighting, to mediate domestic disputes, and to cobble together agreements among hostile constituents. It is not particularly difficult for them to apply these skills internationally. Local officials from St Paul, Minnesota, in the United States, for example, helped mediate a land dispute between its South African sister community of Lawaaikamp, a so-called "black spot," and the neighboring all-white town of George (see Chapter 2 for details). Another example, albeit less successful, occurred in 1991, when several European mayors attempted to use their conflict-resolution skills in Yugoslavia by bringing together mayors from all the republics of the disinte-grating country for dialogue and reconciliation.

Of course, local expertise can be found not only in City Hall but also in a community's non-governmental and private sectors. Some of the best people-centered development occurs when Northerners and Southerners in a given profession – police, teachers, utility managers, doctors, lawyers – exchange technical information, swap success stories, and pursue cooperative projects. In countries with weak or non-existent local governments, such exchanges may be one of the only reliable ways to advance people-centered development.

CDIs Supplement National Initiatives

A final way community action facilitates people-centered development is by offering an avenue for change outside the labyrinths of national bureaucracies.

The most forward-looking communities in a given country are often more interested in people-centered development than are national foreign-policy apparatchiks, for three reasons.

Communities are closer to the people. The first officials to hear and understand popular calls for people-centered development are likely to be at the local level, where connections between people and their politicians are close and personal. Unlike national officials, community politicians are rarely farther than a telephone call or a city council meeting away.

National governments also may be unresponsive because they lack the resources to support thousands of small-scale initiatives. Literally billions of transactions occur every day in the fields of global communication, transportation, finance, trade, and tourism. Central governments can do little more than set ground rules for these transactions and leave the details to other players – citizens, NGOs, churches, corporations, and local governments. There are simply too many conflicts, too many human rights violations, too many undemocratic political practices, too many environmental messes, and too much corporate misbehavior for national governments to manage on their own. When national policy-makers become overtaxed and overextended, communities have a right – indeed, a responsibility – to jump in.

Some national governments view the goals of people-centered development as a threat to their own base of power. They understandably worry that if more people are given power to participate in politics or to redistribute wealth, their own power might be weakened. This is especially true for the practitioners of foreign policy, who traditionally guard their sovereign power jealously and who have very little experience or interest in working with grassroots movements. Communities, in contrast, are likely to adopt CDIs precisely because they increase local power vis-à-vis the national government's.

For all these reasons, at least some communities in a given nation are likely to support people-centered development more quickly and more strongly than national officials. This is not to say that foreign ministries always oppose people-centered development. But even in countries such as the Netherlands and Germany, where national governments underwrite many elements of people-centered development, one can find communities that are willing to go faster and farther. Thus, CDIs can reorient a misguided national development policy and make a good national development policy even better.

• • •

All these advantages of CDIs, of course, are somewhat theoretical. Not every CDI is empowering, innovative, responsive, or effective; some are trivial, misguided, and counterproductive. Nor do all CDIs take advantage of local expertise; some demonstrate local inexperience, ineptitude, parochialism, and corruption. And it is not difficult to imagine CDIs that some day will interfere with or undercut national initiatives supportive of people-centered development.

But the evidence to date suggests that CDIs are more likely than their national counterparts to promote a model of development that is people-centered, multidimensional, and two-way. Once people approach development through specific human relationships instead of abstract macroeconomics, old habits of insensitivity and paternalism become tougher to maintain. Wrong-headed decisions are still possible through CDIs, but there are more opportunities for dialogue, rethinking, and changing course. If nothing else, CDIs are incapable of the kinds of megadisasters caused by, say, the World Bank's efforts to build highways and hydroelectric dams in the Amazon.

Ultimately, the most significant advantage of CDIs is that they tap the wisdom and vision of the people who are being "developed." People may be mistaken about what is in their own interests, but at least the mistakes are their own. As participatory democracy spreads around the world, there is increasing acceptance of its most fundamental principle: that individuals, right or wrong, are the best judges of their own destiny.

CHAPTER 2

Tools

CDIs are tools which communities can use to influence international affairs. They fall into one of ten categories: education, twinning/linking, project support, technical/administrative assistance, campaigning, preferences/sanctions, regulation, institutions, international agreements, and grants. These categories are somewhat artificial, since there are no universally accepted definitions or borderlines between them. Some people categorize every CDI tool as a type of development education on the ground that each CDI raises public awareness and trains participants to ask key questions. Others believe that development education, project support, and technical assistance should be deemed elements of linking programs. Many CDIs clearly fall into more than one category.

What follows is a brief description of each tool, with examples drawn from around the world.

Education

The simplest and most prevalent CDI is awareness-raising. Promoters of public education on North–South issues stress four different goals.

People first must have a *basic understanding* of development and the related issues of security, trade, debt, and the environment. Awareness is a prerequisite for all other CDIs.

Second, they must have the *capacity to ask questions*: Who has power, who doesn't, and why? Who is setting the development agenda? Who benefits from today's order and who suffers? How are global affairs affecting local affairs, and how can communities constructively influence global affairs? Unless people have enough information to think critically, they can hardly be expected to campaign effectively, to start linking projects with real substance, or to know what kinds of technical assistance their counterparts really need.

A third goal for development education is to enhance people's *commitment* to global political change. People-centered development requires more than armchair learning or dropping coins into a tin cup; it requires political participation. Development education therefore helps people understand the links between their own lives and those of others throughout the world. Once people see their own role in the world and recognize their power, they can begin to change their own lives and change the world.

A fourth goal is to provide people with the *skills* necessary to become effective players in international affairs. Speaking a foreign language, showing sensitivity toward another culture, knowing how to organize, and being a good listener are all examples of invaluable skills for a global citizen.

An increasingly important focus for development education is to create a new awareness in the North. One of the submissions from the UNEP–UK Environment and Development Education and Training Group, which provided input to the 1992 United Nations Conference on Environment and Development, states: "Whilst the role of governments and institutions is important, ultimately it is the awareness, understanding, skills, and commitment of each person – the consumers, producers, voters – that will determine how far sustainable development is possible." This view is seconded by Elvia Alvarado, a Honduran peasant activist: "We are not asking for food or clothing or money. We want you with us in the struggle. We want you to educate your people."

Of course, a new awareness also is needed in the South. Moussa Conteh of Sierra Leone believes that more people in the South must understand the legacy of colonialism and unsuccessful Northern development initiatives:

> Development education should be used as an incision tool to remove the cataract in our eyes, so we can have a clear vision. Development education should help us to redeem our dignity and value in our own eyes first, and that should arm us to challenge and fight and restore what we were robbed of as a result of colonization. Development education should instill pride in us to fight for and claim acknowledgement for our contribution to the rest of the world – for example, Black Africa's contribution to the development of Egyptian civilization;…and an East African pilot's help to Vasco da Gama to find the sea route to India.

Most people initially think of development education as a task for primary and secondary schools, universities, and adult-education programs. These institutions are certainly fruitful places for development education to start, especially when they reach young people who are still formulating their world views. The Folk High Schools in Denmark have been educating students to participate in development work for more than 125 years. According to co-founder Christian Kold: "You must awaken people before you pass them information." The city of Amsterdam prepares teaching and learning guides to help secondary school students learn about Managua, the city's partner city in Nicaragua.

If done well, development education empowers both pupils and teachers to act. After development education was introduced into secondary schools in Austria in the 1980s, the students and teachers involved in the programs decided to sponsor special projects and link up with schools in the South. Many of these initiatives received enormous press attention. One Austrian school linking was publicized by a press conference featuring the Austrian prime minister.

Many Italian schools use development education as a springboard for school-to-school linkings. In 1988 a secondary school in Milan linked up with not one but two partners. One was a school in Villa El Salvador, an enterprising, self-organized community on the outskirts of Lima, Peru. The other was a school in Reggio Calabria, a poor community in southern Italy. These three-way links enabled Milan students to compare two different kinds of North–South relations. For a year students in all three schools learned about their partners and communicated with them through letters, questionnaires, and videos. All the children finally met in late 1989.

Development education in Finland similarly opened the door to a wide range of projects. A survey by the Finnish Ministry of Education in 1988 found that 92 of its schools were linked with schools in the South (81 of them in Africa). Some Finnish children have involved themselves in pen-pal correspondence and, in a few instances, exchanges of exhibitions, dispatches of material aid, and visits to the South. Since the late 1960s, Finnish secondary schools have sponsored "Operation Day-Work" campaigns to support "solidarity projects" in the South. Once every two or three years students get a day off school, perform public service work, and donate earnings to these projects. Under this program hundreds of thousands of students have contributed millions of dollars.

Development education in India, found primarily in social work curricula, teaches adults how to become better catalysts for political change. Participants in these classes learn about the principles of people-centered development and the basics of political organizing.

Awareness-raising often goes beyond the classroom. Ever since 1965, when the Food and Agriculture Organization of the United Nations organized a world campaign against hunger, Belgian cities have been raising money for projects in the South through the "11.11.11 Campaign." Named for the moment when an armistice formally ended World War One (November 11, at 11 a.m), the 11.11.11 Campaign is now supported by nearly 250 of the 308 municipalities in Flanders, one of the three regions in Belgium, and has become an occasion for raising public awareness about the South and for fund-raising for projects in the South. In the weeks leading up to November 11, participating municipalities come alive with activities. Festivals and "Third World markets" give Belgians a flavor of Southern food, music, crafts, and goods. The National Center for Development Cooperation, an NGO known as NCOS, has convinced city libraries throughout Flanders to purchase books and house small exhibits on North–South issues; one exhibition currently touring the country discusses the importance of conserving tropical timber. In the small town of Roeselare, a display in the main shopping square dramatized the environmental and trade problems facing developing nations. Brugge has a "Third World Centre" with four staff who produce pamphlets, video tapes, school materials, and exhibitions on North–South issues. Many cities let citizens know about 11.11.11 activities through official town newspapers or magazines, usually distributed free of charge. And Belgian radio and television stations broadcast special 11.11.11 programs.

During the last 15 years development education has increasingly embraced the principles of people-centered development. The old focus on "underdevelopment" has given way to a critical examination of how Northerners exacerbate poverty by maintaining wasteful lifestyles, refusing to cancel unpayable loans, and pushing misguided development projects. Development educators have challenged the verbal and visual depictions of the South as impoverished and incapable of self-reliance. In the UK city of Manchester a local network of teachers has a project on "Images of Africa."

As more immigrant groups settle in Northern communities, development education is being used to fight racism and promote multiculturalism. Development educators try to help people see the "Third World in their midst" by supporting NGOs (such as the Turkish cultural centers in Belgium and the Greek parents' associations located across Europe) that protect the cultural integrity of new immigrants. Following this philosophy, Luxembourg provides a small grant to a community group to preserve the culture of the 5,000 Cape Verdeans living in the city-state.

Local authorities in some countries have co-sponsored multipurpose Development Education Centers (DECs) to help teachers and civil servants engage in public outreach on North–South issues. In the United Kingdom, Reading's International Support Centre provides a platform for speakers from the South and organizes "rapid response meetings" around current events in international affairs (the Gulf War was one of the more hotly debated subjects in recent years). The UK has 40 such DECs. Dutch provinces and municipalities fund 22 Centers for Development Cooperation, so-called "COSsen," with annual grants totaling 1 million guilders ($541,000) and additional grants of 3 million guilders ($1,622,000) from the Dutch National Committee for Development Education (NCO).

Development education can even focus on local officials. The Tingvoll Town Council in Norway has organized special environmental courses for council politicians and administrators. HELLINAS in Greece has held seminars on the Cologne Appeal for mayors, civil servants, and NGOs in Athens, Thessoloniki, Paros, and Rhodes. NCO has sponsored CDI conferences for Dutch elected officials and civil servants.

Linking and Twinning

A second common type of CDI involves a Northern and a Southern community establishing a relationship with each other. The relationship can be formal or informal, and can operate with or without the official endorsement of the local authorities. Depending on where in the world one is, these relationships are called twinnings, sister cities, or sister communities.

Europeans sometimes make a distinction between twinning and linking. Twinning refers to a formal relationship between two communities as a whole, while linking refers to informal relationships between communities and between different entities within the communities such as churches, hospitals, or schools. Thus, Stevenage in the United Kingdom is twinned with Chimkent in Kazakhstan, but the relationship between a school in Stevenage and a school in Chimkent is a linking. Many practitioners, however, use these terms interchangeably, and for simplicity the term "linking" will be used for the remainder of this section.

Jane Knight, until recently the head of linking programs for Oxfam-UK, defines North–South linking as "direct people-to-people contact, leading to equal, mutually beneficial relationships across cultures, with the aim of understanding the reality of each others' lives, and thereby contributing to changes in both their societies – i.e. contributing to each others' development." Even though this definition contains elements that are aspirational rather than descriptive (not all links are equally and mutually beneficial), it captures the key concepts of linking: people-to-people contact, mutual learning, increased understanding, and two-way development.

Perhaps the biggest payoff for participants in linking programs is meeting people. "The close contact with other people which is achieved during a visit," says one Norwegian involved in linking, "is particularly inspiring." Northerners, of course, have long sought personal contact with people in the South, though usually for trade, tourism, missionary work, or slavery. Linking allows a different kind of contact, the chance for people in the North and the South to meet on more equal terms.

Linking also creates a microcosm of North–South relations. It enables people on both sides to put real faces on otherwise abstract international problems. It provides specific opportunities for participants to learn from and to help one another.

One of the virtues of linking is that it can involve people of all ages, even young children, as several Norwegian links demonstrate. In late 1991, 30 students from Nadderud visited two villages in India, Bubaneshwar and Raipur, and they are now raising funds for Indian children to visit Nadderud. Students in seven elementary and secondary schools in Greaker are writing to 2,000 pupils in El Salvador. Bryn's link with Essau in the Gambia led to a remarkable fund-raising drive by fourth graders to buy a cow so that their African counterparts could have fresh milk. The Greverud School in Oppegard runs the "Thanapara Cafe" every week to raise money for projects benefiting children in Thanapara, Bangladesh. The children involved in these linkings stay in touch by exchanging letters, pictures, drawings, cassettes, and videos.

Over the past two decades there has been an explosion of linkings, primarily emanating from the North. Five Northern countries have more than 100 links each with the South: the United Kingdom has 151; the Netherlands has 280 (including 30 formal twinnings); France has 200, primarily with Francophone

Africa; Germany has 600 informal links (including 100 formal twinnings); and the United States has 719 sister cities (including 100 informal ties with Nicaraguan, Salvadoran, and South African communities).

The concept of linking has spread so widely that, as Knight notes, "the question is no longer whether to link but rather: with whom? – with what focus? – and how?" To help answer these questions in the United Kingdom, the United Kingdom One World Linking Association (UKOWLA) was formed in 1985. UKOWLA quickly found itself addressing not just the nuts and bolts of linking but also some tough questions: How can Northern partners recognize and overcome their own racism? How can Northern partners better listen and respond to Southern concerns? What kind of development should linking partnerships be promoting?

Just as development education has begotten linking, linking has begotten development education, as several interesting examples from the United Kingdom attest. Marlborough's link with Gunjur in the Gambia, which gave many English citizens the chance to host or visit Gambians, strengthened the community's intolerance of racism. Knight notes the benefits inuring to the residents of Leamington Spa after welcoming students from Sierra Leone and other parts of Africa into their homes: "Knowledge of the current crisis in Sierra Leone is probably more widespread and accurate in Leamington Spa than in any other British group of people because of the "grapevine" of contacts and friends at the grassroots."

Another example of learning through linking comes from Japan, where the fishing village of Goshiki-Cho gained new insights on how to take better care of the elderly from its ties with an Indonesian fishing village.

Once Lissone, a center for Italian furniture manufacturing and carpentry, formally linked with the region of Man in the Ivory Coast, a wide variety of projects began. Sister nursery schools were established, with children from Man planting trees christened with the names of children from Lissone. The Union of Craftsmen of Monza and Brianza established a bazaar to market arts and crafts from the Ivory Coast and put on carpentry workshops in Man. The Italian State Secondary School for Industry and Commerce provided scholarships for students from the Ivory Coast to learn about sustainable forestry. Teenagers from Lissone started a magazine about student involvement in North–South issues.

Linking has spawned other kinds of CDIs as well. A community in Lower Saxony, Germany, lobbied the European Community to halt the export of pesticides believed to be killing off fish eaten and sold by their partners in the Philippines. A decade-old link between a town in the United Kingdom and a small Asian community motivated the British partners to press Parliament to rein in a multinational logging company that was about to destroy the latter's sacred tribal lands.

Project Support

Twinning and linking invariably sow the seeds for development projects. Austrian communities have helped their linking partners in the South learn vocational skills, dig canals, construct sewage treatment systems, and organize cooperatives. Other Northern communities provide money, volunteers, and technology to build schools, hospitals, roads, and bridges. Following the principles of the Cologne Appeal, many of these projects promote environmental protection and focus on the needs of the poorest people in the South, especially women.

Sometimes Northern communities support Southern projects by contributing money to Northern or Southern NGOs. Take, for instance, the city-state of Bremen in Germany. CDI organizations in Bremen realized that Southern countries can manufacture fertilizer in two ways. The first is to build a large Western-style factory that uses feedstocks of imported oil and chemicals. The second is to use the same amount of money to build biogas digesters for 26,000 villages that can transform cow dung and agricultural wastes into natural fertilizer. The first method consumes vast quantities of energy and requires expensive imports of oil, chemicals, and technology from the West. The second *produces* energy for cooking, requires no imports, and creates 130 times as many jobs. The first has long been promoted by national development agencies and international organizations such as the World Bank. The second has been the centerpiece of Bremen's development cooperation with China, India, and Africa.

Bremen's assistance with biogas projects began in 1979 when it sponsored an international workshop on the topic. Since then, Bremen has co-sponsored two more biogas conferences, financed a technical newsletter called *Biogas Forum*, and supported demonstration projects through the Bremen Overseas Research and Development Association (BORDA). Between 1979 and 1988 Bremen spent DM500,000 ($304,000) to spread biogas technology in Mali, Ethiopia, and Tanzania.

Of course, project work does not always go smoothly. Northerners working in the South often are frustrated by the absence of an institutional infrastructure, roads, maintenance services, tools and equipment, stationery and photocopiers. Effectiveness depends on good preparation and a high level of personal motivation. As Paul van Tongeren of the Netherlands notes, the motto is: "Give us the job and we will make the tools."

But there is a deeper problem that plagues projects: the question of balance. Musa Njiru of Kenya admonished German North–South groups about the pitfalls of project support:

> Uninformed intervention by the North in the South through the project approach in particular often overshadows the real needs and real purpose of cooperation and ought therefore to stop as a matter of urgency. The people

in the North must desist from building dependent attitudes which lead to lack of local initiative and self-respect in the South.

At a minimum, Njiru's criticism underscores why projects should spread skills and help the beneficiaries achieve self-reliance. But it is equally important that Northern communities identify projects in their own backyard with which Southern partners can assist.

Technical and Administrative Assistance

Technical and administrative assistance enables civil servants to share their special expertise and know-how with counterparts abroad. Some of the knowledge that localities have to offer, such as how to build roads or how to design water systems, is of a technical nature. But municipal expertise also exists with respect to "good governance," a concept that encompasses sound planning, efficient administration, and effective leadership.

The International Union of Local Authorities (IULA) began promoting technical cooperation between municipalities in the 1960s and adopted a policy paper on North–South and East–West exchanges in 1988. Adhering to the slogan "Support, don't lead," IULA then organized special courses for municipal officers from developing countries twice a year. (IULA discontinued these courses in 1991, but the Association of Netherlands Municipalities [VNG] plans to resume them.) Similar exchanges were sponsored by the United Towns Organisation, the Council of European Municipalities and Regions (the European section of IULA), the Union of Capital Cities of Ibero-America (which links Spain to Latin America), and Asia Pacific Citynet (an association of 24 cities and eight NGOs in Asia). Some of these initiatives enjoy financial support from bilateral and multilateral donor agencies such as the European Commission, the United Nations Development Programme, and the World Bank.

Two particularly well-organized and well-funded exchange programs have been undertaken by the Federation of Canadian Municipalities (FCM) and by the VNG.

In 1988, with assistance from the Canadian International Development Agency (CIDA), FCM launched its Africa 2000 Program, which funds city-to-city technical exchanges for up to three years. Each participating Canadian city is expected to provide three city administrators or technicians to work briefly in Africa, and to host two or more professionals from its African partner community for three weeks. CIDA provides communities with matching funds of up to $25,000, which they can use to cover expenses, to buy equipment for African partners, and to start up projects. Thus far, 22 Canadian communities have participated.

In 1991 the VNG in the Netherlands began a program to provide Southern partners not only with technical know-how but also with briefings on civil society and local democracy. For up to three months Dutch municipal officers are sent South, and for up to six months municipal officers from the South have city internships in the Netherlands. Dutch participants continue to receive salaries from their cities, while the Ministry of Foreign Affairs covers travel costs. The Ministry also pays municipalities that provide internships a weekly compensation check. At the end of 1991, 60 Dutch municipalities indicated that they wanted to participate in this program.

The VNG also has set up a professional training program involving municipal officers from Eastern Europe. Last year more than one hundred senior officers and fifty local administrators from the East participated. Building on this experience, the VNG now is organizing a program to support trilateral cooperation among Dutch, Nicaraguan, and Czechoslovakian communities. The goal is to raise awareness in all three countries by setting up ten to fifteen North–South–East twinning relationships. With financial support from the Dutch Ministry of Development Cooperation, Czechoslovakian municipalities will transfer technical know-how to urban development projects in Nicaragua.

Erik-Jan Hertogs of the VNG argues that technical and administrative exchanges work best when the emphasis is on mutual learning and not on completing a project. He recommends a series of short visits rather than one lengthy visit, because the longer a foreign civil servant stays, the more inclined he or she will be to take over tasks and the more dependent the municipality in the South will become on outside assistance. Even if stays are short, however, the relationship should be long-term, because the partners need to build up mutual trust and understanding. Finally, Hertogs suggests that Southern civil servants use their Northern partners to get second opinions on their plans.

The late Mr P. van Leeuwen, who was the Dutch coordinator of the technical exchange program between Rotterdam and Jakarta, used to advise participants to follow several golden rules: don't overestimate your possibilities; limit the subject matter of cooperation; involve only your best personnel; keep the exchange independent of commercial interests; make clear agreements; and, above all, be patient and diligent.

Campaigning

A fifth type of CDI is to change the behavior of governments and institutions through persuasion and lobbying, either at home or abroad. One exemplary effort to influence national positions on development has been the North–South Campaign, which has been facilitating a "quadrilogue" among government representatives, parliamentarians, local authorities, and NGOs in a majority of the 27 countries which are members of the Council of Europe. This campaign was originally started as a top-down effort by Strasbourg and by national governments to raise public consciousness on North–South issues, but now the political mechanisms are working in reverse. In Germany, for example, North–South forums have enabled NGOs and local authorities to pass a series of "declarations" in Mainz (1988), Bonn (1990), and Berlin (1991) that have helped shape the direction of national development policy.

Campaign Aid, founded in Ireland in 1987, is a coalition of 38 NGOs lobbying to raise the level of Ireland's Official Development Assistance to the South. A key part of its strategy has been to recruit the support of local elected officials and town councils.

Some of the most successful campaigns in Europe have been organized around environmental issues. In the autumn of 1991 the Christian Labour Movement and a coalition of environmental groups in Flanders launched a campaign entitled "Every Tree Is Worth Two." About two hundred Belgian communities planted 1,500 trees, educated the public about deforestation, and convinced the government to set aside 1 million Belgian francs ($29,000) in the 1992 national budget for environmental protection projects in the South.

Another campaign to fight deforestation has been the Tropical Timber Campaign, which began in the Netherlands in 1989. Two-thirds of the communities in the Netherlands adopted an official policy to reduce consumption of tropical timber in municipal building projects "whenever possible." The campaign gradually spread to other municipalities in Europe and Japan. Sabine Csampai, mayor of Munich, wrote to the governor of Tokyo that "in Munich we have now officially resolved not to use tropical timber in public projects," that "partly because of Japan's proximity to South-East Asian rainforests, the per capita consumption of tropical timber in [Japan] is considerably higher than in Europe," and that therefore Tokyo should consider adopting "resolutions such as ours for the benefit of tropical rainforests and their inhabitants." Tokyo responded favorably, and now local groups are lobbying in 45 Japanese municipalities.

Citizens of St Paul, Minnesota, were able to use campaigning to save the black township of Lawaaikamp from being demolished by the South African authorities. In 1987 St Paul established a sister-community relationship with Lawaaikamp. St Paul council member Bill Wilson traveled to South Africa with the Reverend Oliver White, president of the St Paul Black Ministerial Alliance, and they arranged unprecedented meetings between the elected representatives of Lawaaikamp and officials from George, the neighboring white community that was pushing for the forced removal of Lawaaikamp's citizens. According to a member of the Lawaaikamp Civic Association, "For the first time, [George city officials] came into our house and had tea and talked to people...They showed their preparedness [to try] to find a common solution." Members of the St Paul city council lobbied key members of Congress and the South African embassy, and St Paul high school students barraged Gert Viljoen, the minister of constitutional development and planning, with letters of protest. By November 1989, the government of South Africa agreed to provide an interest-free loan to the city of George to upgrade living conditions in Lawaaikamp and declared the township a Free Settlement Area.

European cities initiated several campaigns concerning Nicaragua. In 1988, at the first European Conference on City Links with Nicaragua, representatives of 150 communities appealed to President Ronald Reagan and Communist Party Chair Mikhail Gorbachev not to intervene militarily in Nicaragua. The conference also established a European Secretariat to lobby the European Commission on Nicaragua policy. When the Sandinistas declared a "state of emergency," several European mayors corresponded and exercised "silent diplomacy" with their counterparts in Nicaragua.

Berkeley's relationship with San Antonio Los Ranchos in El Salvador demonstrates how campaigning on human rights issues can save lives. In January 1989, Salvadoran armed forces arrested Amadeo Lopez, the mayor of San Antonio Los Ranchos, and after charging him with being a guerrilla leader they tortured him for information. In fact, his only crime was leading 900 Salvadoran refugees from a camp in Honduras back to the town, which the army had wanted to keep empty. Loni Hancock, the newly elected mayor of Berkeley, and the city council sent strong statements condemning the capture to national leaders in both El Salvador and the United States. Hancock then met with the Salvadoran consulate general in San Francisco, called the Salvadoran Governmental Human Rights Commission, and urged her congressional representative, Ronald Dellums, to do some arm-twisting with US diplomats in El Salvador. Shortly thereafter, a civil judge in El Salvador pronounced the accusations of the army as having "no merit" and released Lopez.

Campaigns can be directed not only against national governments but also against regional and international authorities. Towns and Development, for example, aims to ensure that the Council of Europe and the European Commission make CDIs a priority in their North–South development policies.

Preferences and Sanctions

One particularly effective campaigning technique is to use the power of the purse. A locality can bestow economic rewards on corporations or governments that are behaving well in North–South relations, or they can punish those that are behaving poorly.

An example of the impact of preferential purchasing comes from the Netherlands, where more than 300 communities and eleven (of twelve) provincial governments are buying "solidarity coffee." So-called "alternative trade" organizations procure coffee beans from small-scale, responsible producers in the South at a slightly higher price to ensure that the growers receive enough revenue to make a decent living. By circumventing middlemen, who usually take a huge share of the profits, alternative traders are able to sell coffee beans to mainstream roasters and distributors at a competitive price. Shoppers can identify solidarity coffee because it bears the "Max Havelaar" seal of approval. After just four years, solidarity coffee has captured over 2 percent of the coffee market in the Netherlands and, along with solidarity tea and cocoa, is being introduced into Belgium, France, Germany, Luxembourg, Switzerland, and the United Kingdom. As a result of the Dutch campaign, low-income coffee farmers are receiving an extra 8 million guilders ($4 million) of income per year. Moreover, in each of the 300 Dutch municipalities where civil servants and city officials now drink solidarity coffee, public debate over the purchasing policy has helped to raise awareness about the inequities facing producers of raw commodities in the South.

Local governments in Europe also have encouraged their constituents to practice preferential purchasing. There are now 500 "Third World shops" in Germany, 300 Wereldwinkels ("world shops") in the Netherlands, and 20 "Third World houses" in Denmark, many of which enjoy the support of local authorities. These stores sell crafts, clothing, and other goods from the South, usually with little or no mark-up in price. Items are purchased from people or cooperatives in the South that pay livable wages and provide decent working conditions. Displays and literature inside the shops educate Northern customers about the makers of the goods, and profits sometimes are used to support local CDIs.

In the mid-1980s the Greater London Council (GLC) helped to fund the Third World Information Network (TWIN) and Twin Trading, firms dedicated to promoting alternative trade between cooperatives and small-scale enterprises in London and their counterparts in the South. Prime Minister Margaret Thatcher abolished the GLC before these efforts could proceed very far, but TWIN Ltd continues as a private promoter of alternative trade. The efforts of TWIN and other alternative trade organizations suggest the promise of creating special trade linkages between the poor in the North and the poor in the South.

Sanctions are essentially the opposite of preferences. By refusing to purchase or to invest in certain countries or companies, a community can persuade them to change their behavior. Perhaps the most successful example of this occurred in the United States, where a total of 27 states, 25 counties, and 101 cities put sanctions on corporations doing business in South Africa (including South African companies). Having a fiduciary duty to invest the pension funds of their public employees, most of these localities decided to reinvest more than $20 billion in "clean" firms with no ties to South Africa. Some communities also refused to do their banking with or to buy goods from companies involved in South Africa. The Port of Wilmington, Delaware, went a step farther and refused to unload any cargoes from South Africa.

Once these sanctions were put into effect, two-thirds of all American companies with ties to South Africa sold off their equity shares and the US Congress passed a Comprehensive Anti-Apartheid Act in 1986, mustering the two-thirds majority needed in both legislative houses to overcome President Reagan's veto. In July 1991 President Bush lifted national sanctions, but in the following year no US company reestablished equity ties with South Africa for fear of triggering state and local sanctions. Community sanctions, in other words, effectively rewrote US foreign policy with respect to South Africa – twice!

In 1975 several Dutch cities convinced Stevin, a major dredging and building firm, to pull out of Chile, shortly after General Augusto Pinochet had overthrown the elected government of Salvador Allende. The head of Stevin, which had signed a $62.5 million contract with Pinochet defended the deal by arguing: "It's normal in Chile to change governments by coup d'etat." The Chilean community in Holland and the Dutch Labor Party were enraged by this comment and called for a boycott. Rotterdam and Haarlem decided to suspend their contracts with Stevin, and other cities were prepared to follow suit. Afraid of losing the more than 50 percent of its business that was dependent on Dutch local governments, Stevin ultimately cancelled its Chilean contract.

The Tropical Timber Campaign, mentioned earlier, is another good example of selective purchasing. Two-thirds of all Dutch municipalities have committed themselves to minimizing the use of tropical timber in city building projects. With the support of the Association of Netherlands Municipalities, the campaign has managed to cut Dutch consumption of tropical timber between 6 and 40 percent. Integral to the campaign have been efforts to convince private architects to stop using tropical timber and to educate the public about the dangers of deforestation through handbooks, pamphlets, newspaper editorials, and city council debates. One concrete result of the campaign is that the national government has agreed to import only sustainably produced tropical timber starting in 1995.

Selective-investment and selective-contracting campaigns often encounter strong legal and political resistance. When 84 municipalities in the Netherlands tried to organize community boycotts against Royal Dutch Shell, which was heavily involved in South Africa, the central government nullified their actions. But subsequent events in the Netherlands suggest that even a "failed" boycott can succeed in raising public awareness and changing the purchasing behavior of individual consumers.

Regulation

While there are not many examples of communities using their regulatory powers to act on North–South issues, what has been done suggests possibilities for future action. Some communities, for example, have passed laws to make modest contributions to stave off global warming and ozone depletion. They have planted millions of trees, limited the use of pesticides, required houses and industries to conform to stringent energy-conservation standards, and put special tolls and taxes on cars to encourage the use of mass transit.

In the United States, where local governments have a great deal of regulatory authority, two dozen cities in the late 1980s banned the local use of chemicals implicated in depleting the earth's ozone layer, such as halons, methyl chloroform, carbon-tetrachloride, and chlorofluorocarbons (CFCs). Denver's ordinance limited sales of all aerosol containers, fire extinguishers, building insulation, and food packaging that use ozone-depleting compounds. It also prohibited any release of CFCs by businesses that use or repair refrigeration equipment, air-conditioners, and automobiles. Long Island's Suffolk County severely restricted the use of polystyrene plastic foam and polyvinyl-chloride grocery bags, and it was later joined by Berkeley, Palo Alto, and Portland. These ground-breaking local initiatives prompted state and national legislators to take the problems posed by CFCs more seriously. In 1989 eight state legislatures moved to regulate CFCs and the US Senate killed a provision in the Clean Air Act that would have halted local and state law-making in the area by an 80-to-16 margin.

Responding to the problems of global migration, a number of cities worldwide have used their regulatory powers to protect refugees from international war zones. In the United States, for example, 27 cities declared themselves "sanctuaries" and ordered their police departments not to cooperate with federal authorities who were seeking to deport refugees from Guatemala and El Salvador.

But not all local regulatory measures are well received by higher authorities. When the Hague and Dordrecht refused to allow *private* architects and builders to use tropical timber (most of the regulations in the Tropical Timber Campaign dealt only with public projects), the Dutch government quashed the measures. Similarly, the US government overturned the city of Oakland's nuclear-free zone, which among other things banned private contractors from working on government nuclear-weapons contracts.

Institutions

Some communities have not been content to implement CDIs on an ad-hoc basis. Instead, they have established public or quasi-public institutions to oversee all their CDIs.

Nearly all the 308 municipalities in Flanders have several interlocking institutions for promoting public awareness on North–South issues: an alderman dedicated to the field, a local advisory board, and public procedures for setting policy. The tasks of the advisory board include coordinating different initiatives, lobbying city council, and pointing out inconsistencies between a city's development policies and its behavior. Sometimes these boards receive formal recognition from the city council, but usually they are independent.

Because the designated alderman in each Flanders town has other responsibilities and because the committee members or board members are volunteers, a number of Belgian cities also hire paid clerks for development cooperation.

These positions go by a variety of names: the "Third World Secretariat" in Louvain, the "Director of the Third World Multi-media Centre" in Brugge, the "Third World Adviser" in Antwerp. Most cities will only hire someone for a short-term position for the annual 11.11.11 Campaign, but they usually hire the same person year after year.

German communities have pioneered several interesting kinds of institutions for CDIs. In 1988 Aschaffenburg (population 60,000) set up a North–South Forum to bring together ten local organizations, including Third World groups, educational institutions, adult education centers, and youth groups. Its mission is to help the groups formulate a common agenda and reduce redundancies. While the forum does not include political parties, it does have close ties to the city council and city administrators. The local government is represented through a contact person who helps secure public spaces for exhibitions, meetings, or advertising. The city provides the forum with DM20,000 ($12,200) per year, half of which financed a dental care facility in Villa Vicensio, Aschaffenburg's partner city in Colombia. It also promotes development education in Aschaffenburg's schools, sponsors North–South lecture series, and holds cultural events such as an annual One World Week.

There are down-sides to Aschaffenburg's forum, too. Members are so overworked from their NGO jobs that they do not have much energy to put into forum projects. The forum also has been unable to respond immediately to unexpected events such as the Persian Gulf War or the recent influx of refugees. And a number of key groups have yet to be adequately included, such as churches, unions, and environmental organizations.

In the small community of Oerlinghausen (population 17,000) in North-Rhine Westphalia, two structures help the city government sort out North–South issues: a network of local environmental and Third World groups; and an advisory board comprising five members of the network, one representative from each of the four political parties on the town council, and a city administrator. Recommendations from the advisory board automatically become action items for the city council.

Using these structures, Oerlinghausen put together a public education campaign in 1990 on the theme of "water is life – here and in the Third World." To give a Northern perspective on the ecological importance of water, the town commemorated the opening of a new sewage plant with guided tours and theater performances. To give a Southern perspective, it focused public attention on an irrigation project in Burkina Faso, which was originally put together by the people of Lemgo, a neighboring German town, and Lemgo's twin city in France. Oerlinghausen incorporated music and dance from Africa into the festivities and invited the ambassador from Burkina Faso.

A third institutional model in Germany is provided by the State Office for Development Cooperation in Bremen. As part of his official business, the director of the office, Gunther Hilliges, has played a leading role in writing and disseminating the Cologne Appeal, setting up the North–South "quadrilogue" structure in Germany, organizing networks of Southern partners in Africa and India, and bringing North–South and East–West partners into new triangular, North–South–East relationships.

In the United Kingdom several overlapping organizations have been promoting CDIs. NGOs such as the United Kingdom One World Linking Association (UKOWLA), the National Association of Development Education Centres (NADEC), and Oxfam-UK have played important roles in getting cities interested in linking and development education. Another important supporter of these CDIs has been the Local Government International Bureau (LGIB), the official conduit between UK local governments and international organizations such as the International Union of Local Authorities (IULA) and the Council of European Municipalities and Regions (CEMR). In 1990 LGIB received three years of funding – £50,000 ($89,000) per year – from the British Overseas Development Administration to set up a "developing countries section." Working closely with national agencies and with NGOs such as Oxfam-UK, LGIB has been able to help local authorities improve and expand their North–South links, set the agenda for the United Nations Conference on the Environment and Development, prepare technical-training programs for developing countries, and design development-education programs. Other kinds of CDIs have enjoyed national coordination as well.

Paul van Tongeren of the Dutch National Committee for Development Education (NCO) urges municipalities in the Netherlands to demonstrate their commitment to CDIs by taking the following six steps: (1) after local elections put a paragraph on development cooperation into a *plan* that guides municipal policy over the next four years; (2) prepare a detailed *policy paper* for the town council on development cooperation; (3) appoint *the mayor or an alderman* to be responsible for municipal activity in the field of development cooperation; (4) hire or appoint a *civil servant* who is responsible for improving and implementing the city's CDI policy on a day-to-day basis; (5) establish a CDI *platform* on which officials and community groups can cooperate; and (6) create a line-item in the *budget* for development cooperation.

A majority of the 650 towns in the Netherlands carry out at least some of these recommendations. One out of three Dutch communities includes a paragraph in their municipal policy plans, two out of three have a policy paper and an elected official taking responsibility for CDIs, 150 have a civil servant devoting at least one day a week to CDIs, half have a formal platform, and 100 spend at least a guilder per capita on CDIs.

Several Dutch cities now prepare a "Clover Four" matrix for CDIs. On one axis is a list of CDI tools. On the other is a roster of the major subjects for CDIs in the Netherlands: development cooperation, peace, South Africa, and the environment. The matrix serves as a checklist to examine systematically what the city has done – and still can do – in international affairs.

International Agreements

Sometimes development initiatives come in the form of agreements between municipalities in different countries. Perhaps the most common pacts have been between communities whose countries share a border. US and Mexican local governments, for example, have agreements to maintain common roads and bridges, to patrol for illegal immigration or drug smuggling, to assign television and radio frequencies, and to manage shared water or energy resources.

Intermunicipal agreements also manifest themselves in the form of ongoing organizations. The International Union of Local Authorities and the United Towns Organization are both consortia of communities addressing development problems. As communities become more sophisticated in foreign affairs, more international consortia probably will emerge to deal with specific development problems. In 1991 several hundred cities from 40 countries formed the International Council for Local Environmental Initiatives (ICLEI) to promote municipal cooperation on such issues as solid waste disposal and reductions of carbon-dioxide emissions.

Grants

A final type of CDI is where a community serves as a foundation and provides grants to non-governmental organizations (NGOs). It is worth noting that an NGO is capable of helping with all kinds of CDIs. It can undertake education, research, and campaigning. It can take on responsibility for linking or project support. It can gather information on corporate misbehavior which municipalities can then use to regulate, boycott, or divest from egregious offenders. And it can become an active part of community institutions and international institutions. For all these activities, local authorities can, and do, underwrite NGOs.

Generally, European local authorities have a stronger tradition of providing grants to NGOs than do local governments elsewhere. The Bremen State Office for Development Cooperation, for example, spends several million deutsche marks per year on grants to a number of local NGOs. It earmarks DM35,000 ($21,300) annually for the Bremen Information Center for Human Rights and Development, a consortium of NGOs which was responsible for 88 different North–South events in 1990. In the United Kingdom local authorities also support NGOs carrying out development education, linking, refugee assistance, and nuclear-free campaigns.

• • •

These ten CDI tools define the range of possibilities communities have at their disposal to influence North–South development cooperation. Just what tool or tools a community chooses will depend on its legal powers and political inclinations, which vary significantly from country to country. The history of CDIs suggests that a community using even one of these tools, if it uses it well, can exert dramatic influence on international affairs, as the success stories in the next chapter underscore.

CHAPTER 3

Issues

In recent years thousands of communities have used CDIs to protect the earth's environment, to promote human rights, to end civil war in Nicaragua, to weaken apartheid, to improve East–West relations, and to initiate South–South relations. The achievements of these initiatives suggest what may be possible in the future as more local governments, NGOs, and community groups join the CDI movement.

Environmental Protection

Every community is part of the global environment. Its policies influence how much smoke and carbon-dioxide is belched into the air, how many PCBs and heavy metals are dumped into the water, and how much solid waste is produced. A community also has the power to push (or require) its citizens to protect the environment: to recycle wastes, to reuse materials, to conserve energy and water, to protect endangered species, to use fewer materials for city construction projects, to rely on bicycles and mass transit, and to heighten local ecological consciousness. US communities are now spending half of their municipal budgets on environmental management, and Danish communities are dedicating over 90 percent. This suggests why one of the most popular missions for CDIs is to protect and to restore the earth's environment.

US communities acted on many international ecological problems long before the national government did. In 1982 New York State brought together representatives from 21 states and five Canadian provinces for a conference on acid rain at the World Trade Center. In 1983 more than a hundred New England communities, in coordination with NGOs in Canada, passed resolutions petitioning the US government for reductions in industrial emissions from factories in the Midwest. In 1986 officials of the states of Minnesota and North Dakota joined forces with the neighboring Canadian province of Manitoba to coordinate a lobbying campaign against US plans to store high-level radioactive waste in northern Minnesota.

US cities have taken the initiative to reduce their contribution to global warming. Los Angeles is planting 5 million seedlings to absorb carbon-dioxide and has written letters to the city's 14 sister cities to encourage them to enact similar programs.

Phoenix plans to put a million new trees in the ground by 1995. Dade County recently began "Project Releaf" to reforest low-income areas of Miami.

Over 150 European municipalities, including 75 from the Netherlands and 20 from Austria, are fighting global warming through the Climate Alliance. Participating Northern cities have committed themselves to cut carbon-dioxide emissions in half by the year 2010 through energy conservation, mass transit, and selective purchasing (they will not, for example, buy products that contain CFCs or tropical hardwood). These cities also are providing financial and legal assistance to South American NGOs and indigenous peoples to survey, demarcate, and protect the Amazon rainforest.

Another European initiative to save rainforests, described earlier, is the Tropical Timber Campaign. Two-thirds of Dutch cities and all the cities in one of the federal states of Austria, among others, have agreed to stop using precious hardwoods from the South for public projects.

A long-term goal for communities dedicated to environmental preservation is to become self-sufficient on local food, energy, water, wood, and minerals. To achieve this level of sustainability, Denmark has supported pilot studies in nine communities to see how far they can go in becoming "green municipalities." Each community has programs for environmental education, nature conservancy, energy and water efficiency, recycling, an ecological youth corps, and green purchasing. A similar program has been underway in Davis, California, for more than a decade. Today Davis boasts more bicycles than cars, more gardens than lawns, tough energy efficiency standards for buildings, and a recycling program in which 70 percent of its 50,000 inhabitants voluntarily participate.

In the Netherlands local education campaigns occur every year between April 22 (Earth Day) and June 5 (World Environment Day). Under the banner of "Working Together for a Cleaner World," hundreds of Dutch cities issue declarations or conduct classes on problems such as climate change, energy inefficiency, traffic congestion, solid waste disposal, and deforestation.

The Dutch government recently invited four people from the South to assess the country's ecosystems and provide recommendations for cleaning them up. The team – which included an Indonesian director of an environmental organization, a Tanzanian agronomist, an Indian sociologist, and a Brazilian undersecretary of state for culture in the state of Rio de Janeiro – spent six weeks touring the country and meeting with 40 people who represented every walk of Dutch life. The analysts from the South ultimately called on the Dutch to reverse "overdevelopment" by driving fewer cars, raising fewer animals, and cutting down on wasteful packaging.

In Colombia, a country racked by debt, poverty, drug lords, and violence, the Green Campaign has attempted to revitalize the nation's 1,050 municipalities and transform them into launching pads for environmental CDIs. The campaign was started by Margarita Marino de Botero in 1983, when she was serving as the director general of the National Institute for Natural Resources and the Environment (INDERENA). Botero challenged municipal governments, community groups, and NGOs to form Green Councils to restore local ecosystems. She also encouraged communities to create greenhouses for local reforestation and to educate the public on the destructive impacts of environmental mismanagement and social injustice. Within two years INDERENA had spread millions of seeds and thousands of educational brochures throughout the country, and more than 80 percent of the country's municipalities were participating. The symbol of the movement – a sapling with one green leaf waving like a flag – became visible across the country. More recently the Green Campaign has established three other important institutions: a Green College, which is an open university focusing on environmental protection, sustainable development, global peace, and participatory democracy; a Green Center, which trains rural leaders, city council members, and ecological organizers; and a Green Foundation, which fields 20 teams of lawyers, journalists, teachers, and scientists to improve the quality of Colombia's local governments.

Another recent development is the emergence of the International Council for Local Environmental Initiatives (ICLEI), headquartered in Toronto, Canada, and in Freiburg, Germany. With several hundred members worldwide – including prominent cities in Australia, Brazil, Canada, Germany, Netherlands, Norway, the Philippines, Senegal, Sierra Leone, United Kingdom, United States, and Zimbabwe – ICLEI is finding the best environmental-protection policies and technologies and disseminating them to other cities. Its current focus is to reduce urban carbon-dioxide emissions, but it plans to address other ecological problems as well. Thanks to intensive lobbying by ICLEI, the United Nations Conference on Environment and Development included the following language in Agenda 21: "Indigenous people and their communities, and other local communities, have a vital role in environmental management and development because of their knowledge and traditional practices." Now ICLEI, working with representatives from the United Nations Commission on Sustainable Development, International Union of Local Authorities (IULA), United Towns Organisation, the World Association of Major Metropolises, and the Summit of the World's Major Cities, is helping communities prepare their own local Agenda 21.

In 1991 IULA adopted a Declaration on Environment, Health, and Lifestyle which calls on local governments to integrate the values of environmental quality, human health, biological diversity, and cultural diversity in all decisions regarding planning, setting standards, budgeting, economic development, and public education. The declaration also endorses the following principles: that protection of the environment requires an end to poverty; that polluters should pay for the ecological damage they cause; that the public has a right to environmental information; and that, because of differences in wealth, Northern communities must assume greater responsibility for global clean-up than Southern communities.

Human Rights

Agreeing that there are certain fundamental liberties and entitlements that must be universally respected, communities have become important advocates for human rights. Municipalities have pressed foreign governments to release prisoners of conscience, lobbied against foreign aid for nations with records of barbarism, and "mobilized shame" against regimes guilty of practicing capital punishment, torture, or genocide.

Actually, the long list of human rights protected by the Universal Declaration of Human Rights, which was adopted by the United Nations in 1948, suggests that *most* CDIs can be considered human-rights initiatives. Article 25, for example, states:

> Everyone has the right to a standard of living adequate for the health and well-being of himself and of his family, including food, clothing, housing, and medical care and necessary social services, and the right to security in the event of unemployment, sickness, disability, widowhood, old age or other lack of livelihood in circumstances beyond his control.

A growing number of mayors and city council members have taken on human-rights causes. The mayor of Delft in the Netherlands recently planted trees in a public ceremony to persuade the Syrian government to free a number of physicians who had been imprisoned without a fair trial. When violence erupted in Soviet Armenia in 1988, California Governor George Deukmejian, himself Armenian, wrote to General Secretary Mikhail Gorbachev pleading for a non-violent resolution of the ethnic conflict. The city council of Teaneck, New Jersey, supported an Amnesty International campaign calling on the Brazilian government to investigate the murder of several prominent environmentalists and trade-union workers who had been opposing development of the Amazon. Jack Rendler, Campaign Director for Amnesty International-USA, estimates that there have been "one or two hundred" instances in which human-rights organizers have recruited mayors or city councils.

Some local officials have gone beyond writing letters and passing resolutions. In April 1989 Mayor Larry Agran of Irvine, California, and California State Senator Art Torres traveled to Vietnam to lobby for the release of 30 men whose families had fled Vietnam at the end of the war and then resettled in Orange and Los Angeles counties. The California politicians met with the Vietnamese minister of justice and foreign minister, and by December the first "good faith" release occurred, enabling Thu D. Duong to emigrate to the United States. After spending 14 years as a political prisoner separated from his wife and nine children, Duong said, "Without the help of the people of the United States, especially Larry Agran, I could never have gotten here."

One of the most important human-rights issues facing communities today is the treatment of refugees. In recent years millions of Southerners have entered the United States to flee poverty (Mexicans), environmental disasters (sub-Saharan Africans), wars (Salvadorans, Nicaraguans), and repression (Guatemalans, Haitians). The dramatic collapse of the Warsaw Pact opened the doors for a massive migration of Eastern Europeans to come west. The economic and social dislocations caused by refugees unleashed feelings of racism and intolerance felt most profoundly by those in the South. In Germany, even though recent immigrants have been primarily Poles, Czechs, Slovaks, or Russians, attacks by skinhead and neofascist gangs have been directed against refugees from Africa and the Middle East. The Iron Curtain that once divided East from West is now being replaced by a barbed wire fence along the North–South divide.

The refugees coming north and west are a poignant reminder of why no community can ignore the issues of global development. CDIs give municipalities an opportunity to address the root causes of immigration, as well as to respond humanely to the immediate problem of caring for and protecting refugees.

The United Kingdom, especially the city of London, is now struggling to absorb immigrants from "New Commonwealth" countries such as the West Indies, Pakistan, and India, plus displaced people from Kurdistan, Eastern Europe, and the former Soviet Union. With no national strategy for providing housing or other social services for refugees, British local governments and NGOs such as the Refugee Council have stepped in to fill the void. British local authorities are now spending £60 million ($108 million) per year to house the 10 percent of refugees who qualify as "priority homeless" – that is, people with physical or mental disabilities, families with children, and the elderly. (Most refugees, however, are healthy, single men and therefore are unprotected by these programs.)

Through the London Boroughs Grants Scheme (LBGS) a number of local authorities in the city have pooled funds to provide more than £1 million ($1,790,000) to NGOs assisting refugees. Representatives of these NGOs, in turn, meet every six to eight weeks in an umbrella group called the Refugee Working Party. Some boroughs provide additional grants to community organizations, and eight have created their own Refugee Working Parties involving NGO representatives and civil servants. One successful example of NGO cooperation with local authorities is the Korczak House in South London, which receives funding from several boroughs to take care of the needs of nine refugee children from Eritrea, Ethiopia, and Uganda. But everyone acknowledges that these efforts are not meeting the needs of most refugees.

In 1988 the city of Leiden in the Netherlands launched a campaign called "Leiden: City of Refugees." Leiden officials tried to curb prejudice and racism against immigrants by reminding its inhabitants of the city's history of protecting refugees: at one time two-thirds of its population were refugees, and 70 percent of the current population are descended from refugees.

Some local governments have tried to protect refugees by challenging national deportation policies. As noted earlier, 27 US cities declared themselves sanctuary and refused to cooperate with federal authorities that were seeking to return

Salvadoran and Guatemalan refugees back to the war zones from which they had fled. In 1985 the Dutch city of Enschede formally protested the justice minister's decision to deport four refugees who had been living there. More recently, when the Dutch government asked the city of Zeewolde to erect a fence around a park where asylum-seekers were encamped, the city refused on the grounds that refugees should not be treated as prisoners.

For almost any human-rights issue, communities can play a valuable role in educating and mobilizing the public. The Dutch city of Alkmaar provided every one of its schools with curriculum materials on the rights of refugees. Other city councils in the Netherlands have supported human-rights causes through resolutions, grants, campaigns, purchasing preferences, or divestment. In 1988, 25 Dutch municipalities passed resolutions demanding that European governments adhere to Amnesty International's principles concerning the just treatment of asylum-seekers.

Whether cities should cut off contacts with human-rights violators is often a matter of considerable local debate. Amsterdam decided to sever its ties with Jakarta after the Indonesian government executed several prominent communist leaders. This decision was a consequence of the city's "Criteria for International Development Cooperation Programmes," one of which mandates that "existing relationships shall be reconsidered if the assistance rendered is in itself contributing to violation of human rights, or, if it constitutes an important support to an oppressive regime."

A different approach to human-rights violations was taken by some American cities linked with China. About half of the US–Chinese sister-city programs responded to the Tiananmen Square massacre in 1989 by *strengthening* their ties. Their rationale was to keep channels of communication open so that they could bring human-rights concerns to the attention of Chinese authorities. Continued sister-city relations also could enable Americans to remain in contact with dissidents and other human-rights advocates. And they could facilitate donations of personal computers, Walkmans, fax machines, and photocopiers – technologies that, over time, will erode the Chinese government's monopoly on information and debate.

Arjan Agema of the Amnesty International Dutch Section notes:

> What is at stake here is not so much a choice between two options, but defining the point at which the positive effects of a relationship on the activities of the other party changes into justification of their human-rights violations. The search for this line can sometimes be very difficult.

Anti-apartheid

Ever since apartheid was made the official policy of South Africa, black community groups and NGOs in the country have struggled to dismantle it. But it was not until the late 1970s that NGOs and communities throughout the North joined these anti-apartheid campaigns. Responding to calls from the African National Congress and others to put pressure on the white regime in Pretoria, local authorities and NGOs decided to weaken apartheid in South Africa through a combination of sticks and carrots, wielded in that order. Two of the most successful campaigns occurred in the Netherlands and in the United States.

Dutch towns began opposing apartheid through awareness-raising measures. In 1983 Amsterdam stripped some of its streets and squares of their Boer names and rechristened them with appellations such as Luthuli, Biko, and Mandela. Two years later the city council of Deventer banned the use of South African goods at municipal events and urged the public not to buy South African products.

Because the Dutch actually use very few South African products, debate soon focused on whether to boycott Dutch companies with substantial investments in South Africa, such as Royal Dutch Shell. In October 1987 the cities of Amsterdam, Arnhem, the Hague, Groningen, and Waddinxveen organized a municipal anti-apartheid conference to weigh the merits of local sanctions. Just prior to the meeting, the Dutch government stated flatly that it would not tolerate a boycott. This convinced conference participants of the need for coordinated and concerted action. Nine months later, 20 Dutch cities founded Local Authorities Against Apartheid (LOTA), headquartered in the Hague, and within a year LOTA's membership grew to 80 cities. In many cases the decision to join LOTA was approved by council members from all political parties.

In early 1988 Hilversum defied the government and refused to accept a bid from Shell for municipal rolling stock. Shell complained to the government, and the cabinet promptly overruled Hilversum's action. LOTA then recommended that its members use a positive-preference strategy: rather than boycott firms with ties to South Africa, cities should give special consideration to firms with no such ties. This time 22 city councils acted in unison so that none would be singled out for punishment (as Hilversum had been). The government agreed to meet with local leaders in January 1990, but that meeting and another one in May failed to produce a compromise. The government summarily nullified the 22 positive-preference policies.

LOTA's efforts to organize a municipal boycott ultimately failed, but the battle drew enormous television and press coverage and helped raise public awareness about apartheid. In early 1990 LOTA decided to change tactics. After meeting with several civic associations near Johannesburg, LOTA adopted a general platform to promote people-to-people contacts with black South Africans. LOTA, which then became a part of the Association of Netherlands Municipalities, decided to provide local governance skills to the leaders of the civics. For example, the Hague sent civil servants specializing in housing policy to Wattville, and citizens of the Hague became symbolic members of the civic by paying an annual fee. LOTA also recruited Dutch cities for new partnerships by distributing newsletters and holding a conference in early 1991. This time, the central government not only supported LOTA's plans, it provided funding.

The evolution of anti-apartheid CDIs in the United States was similar to that in the Netherlands, with one twist: because the national government never explicitly preempted state and local sanctions, they were legally upheld. The first US cities divested from firms doing business in South Africa in the late 1970s; by the mid-1980s more than seventy cities and twenty states had done so. As noted earlier, this movement was so powerful that it convinced Congress to end President Reagan's policy of "constructive engagement." The US State Department quietly supported a conservative challenge to Baltimore's divestment ordinance, but it never formally joined the lawsuit. The Justice Department, espousing the conservative philosophy of "states' rights," believed that localities should be able to invest and enter contracts with any companies they chose.

The US sanctions movement was orchestrated primarily by Transafrica and the American Committee on Africa, two NGOs located on the East Coast. A completely different approach was taken on the West Coast by a South African ex-patriate named Louis Freedberg in 1987. Freedberg's US–South Africa Sister Community Program, which linked US cities with the civics, was initially greeted with skepticism by the sanctions community. But its accomplishments, such as saving Lawaaikamp from destruction, gradually won the respect of anti-apartheid activists. Today, there are ten US cities linked with civics, with most of them providing technical assistance and moral support.

While these activities were occurring in the North, NGOs and community groups within South Africa were preparing for the end of white rule. The civic associations within the black townships effectively became the local governments to which most of the community turned for leadership.

Solidarity with Nicaragua

One of the most successful examples of CDIs is the solidarity network that developed between Nicaragua and cities in the North. After the Sandinistas overthrew the tyrannical dictatorship of General Anastasio Somoza-Debayle in 1979, Western European communities formed more than 200 links with Nicaragua and American communities formed 86 links. Only about a quarter of these were formally recognized by city councils in the North, but most enjoyed at least the informal support of the mayor and city council members.

City links with Nicaragua had two objectives: to assist with specific development projects, and to raise Northern awareness about development problems in the Third World generally and in Nicaragua in particular.

Many Northerners admired the Sandinistas for toppling a repressive regime through a mass uprising and for attempting to create a new kind of state system, at least initially, that avoided the pitfalls of both capitalism and socialism. Here was a popular revolution with a humane face that was following its own path to development and that could become a model for the poor throughout the world. Northern supporters of the Sandinistas, many of them young and idealistic, wanted to express their "solidarity" with the Nicaraguan people by making practical contributions to the country's development.

Another motivation of the solidarity movement was to stop the United States from waging its covert war against the Sandinistas. President Ronald Reagan spent most of his presidency trying to dislodge the Sandinistas by arming and supporting the contra rebels and by pressuring international financial institutions such as the World Bank to cut off loans to Nicaragua. Local groups countered by using their municipal links to publicize war atrocities and to protest the Reagan administration's aggressive policies (in Southern and Central Europe, city councils took the initiative).

The Sandinistas warmly welcomed the solidarity movement (for further explanation, see the Nicaragua country report in Appendix I). A vast network of people-to-people contacts and city-to-city relationships fit well with Nicaragua's foreign policy of non-alignment. It also dovetailed with Nicaragua's effort to decentralize power and to strengthen local democracy, which was formalized in the Municipalities Act of 1988.

Solidarity links with Nicaragua typically had four components. First, Northerners provided financial, technical, and volunteer support for projects in their partner city. These projects, aimed at strengthening social and physical infrastructure, were overseen by Nicaraguan municipalities (in part because there were few Nicaraguan NGOs). Second, Northern organizers used the links to provide their constituents with information about Nicaragua, the contra war, and development challenges in the South. Human relationships constituted a third component that enabled Northerners and Nicaraguans to develop respect for one another and to share technical information. As Ronald van der Hijden of the National Council on Netherlands–Nicaragua City Linking notes, "Many Europeans experienced...the problems that Nicaraguans had to overcome in their daily struggle for their own development. This instilled in [the Europeans] a strong motivation to continue their activities for many years." Finally, links were used to mobilize political support for Nicaragua. The debates in European and American city councils over whether to endorse a link aroused public interest and sympathy.

The results of these links were impressive. Thousands of Europeans and Americans traveled to Nicaragua, learned the realities of development in the South, and had personal experiences that changed their lives. Hundreds of millions of dollars were raised for projects in Nicaragua, which not only helped to relieve poverty but also strengthened the country's municipal institutions and civil society. This assistance became especially important when Hurricane Joan caused more than $1 billion of damage in Nicaragua in October 1988. The city of Tucson, Arizona, responded to the disaster by airlifting to Managua and Bluefields 30 tons of aid worth $150,000, including a school bus stuffed with medicines, bike parts, school supplies, tools, and solar photovoltaic panels.

Another direct outcome of the solidarity movement was increased public support for Nicaragua and greater opposition to the US-supported contra war. In the Netherlands, even though national members of the ruling Christian Democratic Party endorsed the US policy, local members of the party (who were mayors, aldermen, and councilors) traveled to Nicaragua, supported linking projects, and became active participants in the solidarity movement. Similarly, many state legislators from Wisconsin and Minnesota who were members of President Reagan's Republican Party spoke out against contra war.

The solidarity movement provided an important base for building opposition to the contras. More than 150 Dutch city councilors signed a declaration against US policies that was presented to the US ambassador in the Netherlands. In January 1988, 32 American mayors called a press conference and demanded a cutoff of military aid for the rebels. Sister-city programs enabled other mayors to travel to Nicaragua with newspaper editors, businessmen, and opinion leaders, all of whom returned with stories dramatically at odds with the information put out by the Reagan administration. These witnesses provided the American people, according to political columnist Alexander Cockburn, with "a level of knowledge and of direct experience with Nicaragua that no amount of thunder from [Undersecretary of State] Elliott Abrams and the others can dispel." Because of this movement, US public opinion remained against contra aid by a margin of two to one, forcing the US Congress to cut off contra aid in February 1988.

Some of the European participants in Nicaraguan linking projects created special foundations and associations that worked alongside solidarity groups and involved politicians and opinion leaders holding a broad range of political viewpoints. These politically moderate organizations did not endorse the Sandinista Party or the FSLN per se, but supported the right of Nicaraguans to choose their own development path without outside interference. During the 1990 elections, solidarity groups promoted local democratization and monitored the elections for fairness.

The Europeans institutionalized their links in several ways. National coordinating offices were set up in Belgium, Germany, the Netherlands, and the United Kingdom. In 1985 the city of Evry in France, with support from the United Towns Organisation (UTO), met with the four other European towns which like itself were linked with Esteli, Nicaragua: Bielefeld (Germany), Delft (Netherlands), St Feliu de Llobregat (Spain), and Sheffield (United Kingdom). In 1988 the city of Amsterdam, UTO, and several other NGOs held the first "European Conference on City Links with Nicaragua," which was attended by more than 350 representatives of cities, NGOs, and town associations from 14 Western European countries, Australia, the United States, and Nicaragua. The conference helped to create small groups to coordinate the work of Northern cities linked with Managua, Leon, Masaya, Matagalpa, Chinandega, Corinto, Nandaime, Condega, San Carlos, and Regio IV. It also established an information center in Amsterdam, which, thanks to funding from the European Community, published a regular newsletter and organized meetings to coordinate European–Nicaraguan initiatives.

The solidarity movement with Nicaragua demonstrated that local authorities could undertake foreign-policy initiatives that were at odds with those taken by their national governments. The mayor of Amsterdam, Ed van Thijn, created a stir in 1984 when he signed an agreement of cooperation with Mayor Santos of Managua. Two weeks earlier the Dutch minister for development cooperation had informed the Nicaraguan government that the Netherlands would be cutting back support for the country. Ultimately, the Dutch government conceded that Amsterdam had the right to establish its own relations with Nicaraguan officials.

Since the elections of 1990, when the Sandinistas were voted out of power nationally and in many municipalities, some of the European and American city links have been disbanded. But linking continues with communities such as Leon and Jalapa, where the Sandinistas still control the city councils. And even with many UNO-run cities, Northern organizers have maintained ties, though the transition has not always been smooth. The new UNO leaders of Managua dropped their formal relationships with Seattle and Madison and set up a relationship with Miami, where 100,000 conservative Nicaraguan exiles live. Seattle and Madison responded by continuing their work with Managua's churches, child-development centers, schools, and youth groups. Norwalk, Connecticut, helped broker a merger between the old Sandinista sister-city committee in Nagarote and a new UNO committee.

Ronald van der Hijden argues that the Nicaraguan solidarity movement is as relevant as ever. The political situation in Nicaragua is still quite fluid. With the UNO coalition fragmenting and with the Sandinistas experiencing "tropical perestroika," Northerners of any political viewpoint can find plenty of opportunities for partnership. Certainly, the *need* for Northern support has never been greater. Poverty and unemployment are on the increase, and Nicaragua's local governments, coping with the impacts of structural adjustment, are desperate for the most basic kinds of technical assistance.

East–West Relations

Communities in the West began to reach out to their counterparts in the East in the early 1980s, when détente between the United States and the Soviet Union broke down. Careless talk about winning a limited nuclear war in Europe and the largest buildup of military forces in history prompted peace activists throughout the West (as well as many in the East) to do whatever they could to ease the superpower confrontation.

Initially, communities on both sides of the Atlantic launched campaigns against nuclear weapons. In Europe millions took to the streets to halt the deployment of the Pershing II and cruise missiles (the so-called "Euromissiles"), while in the United States 900 cities passed resolutions pressing for a "bilateral, verifiable freeze" of the arms race. About 4,500 communities in 23 countries also declared themselves "nuclear-free." In most cases these nuclear-free localities simply enunciated their abhorrence of nuclear weapons, but sometimes they initiated ambitious public-education campaigns. Half the 180 nuclear-free zones in the United States actually made any nuclear-weapons work a criminal offense. In Chicago, for example, anyone found working on a nuclear-weapons contract within city limits can be fined $1,000 per day. A dozen US communities also refused to invest in or buy products from firms involved in the manufacture of nuclear weapons.

Gradually, however, communities in the West came to recognize the limits to the anti-weapons protests. The campaigns for nuclear-free zones were divisive and victory often was achieved by the thinnest of margins. Peace activists came to conclude that it was necessary to address the basic cause of the arms race – the Cold War. Only by replacing East–West enmity with a more constructive relationship, they reasoned, could the arms race finally be halted and reversed.

In the United States a robust "citizen diplomacy" movement took shape, some of it channeled through US–Soviet sister-cities. After the Soviet Union invaded Afghanistan in 1979, five of the six existing US–Soviet sister-city relationships were suspended. The US-based Sister Cities International (SCI) and the Soviet counterpart organization, both fearing the consequences of supporting exchanges in hostile times, refused to establish new ties. But as interest in reaching out to the East increased, many US cities decided to circumvent the official organizations. By 1988, 30 US cities established relations with Soviet cities. Realizing that they were about to miss the boat, SCI and the Soviets jumped aboard.

Many US cities that twinned with Soviet cities faced denunciations by "anti-communists" in the State Department, on newspaper editorial boards, and on city councils. But the whole point of these relationships was to confront Americans" hatred of all things Soviet and to replace the name-calling and saber-rattling with dialogue and constructive cooperation. The movement was more successful than anyone could have predicted. By the time of the failed coup in the Soviet Union, US communities had established 75 officially recognized sister-city relationships with Soviet cities and 50 more were in some stage of formation.

As the US–Soviet sister-cities movement matured, it focused less on cultural and friendship activities and more on technical exchange and trade. This influenced the trajectory of US sister-city ties with Eastern Europe, which became commonplace after the Berlin Wall fell in 1989. With the Cold War over, US cities established business ties and trained elected officials and civil servants from the East (principally Poland), this time with the full support of SCI and the US Conference of Mayors.

Western European twinnings with the East had a different character. They brought together social and political groups and promoted human rights and civil society. Twinning organizers were treated unfavorably by some East Bloc authorities, but they were welcomed in countries like Hungary and Poland that were enjoying the influence of Mikhail Gorbachev's policies of *glasnost* and *perestroika*.

Germany actually started twinning with the East long before Gorbachev came to power. Inspired by Chancellor Willy Brandt's policy of "Ostpolitik," West German cities began linking with Eastern Europe in the 1970s. Between 1982 and 1987, as the peace movement in Europe gathered strength, the number of West German partnerships with Eastern Europe doubled. But not all West Germans were pleased. By the time Saarlouis and Eisenhuttenstadt established the first link between West and East German cities, public opinion was split on whether or not the tie was desirable. Nevertheless, when West German officials tried to scuttle Wiesbaden's partnership with Wroclaw in Poland, it wound up increasing public awareness and interest in East–West twinning, which was one of the main objectives of those promoting the relationship.

Between 1986 and 1989, 60 municipal links were formed between the two Germanys. Although the East German government tried to control them, grassroots contacts and cooperation proceeded further than officials had anticipated. During the summer of 1989 several East German cities such as Leipzig continued their ties with the West despite orders from Erich Honiker to cut them off. As Beate Wagner from the University of Berlin argues, the "local cooperation structures proved to be more stable than national policies."

Some twinning activities continued once the two Germanys began to unify; for example, contacts between East and West German schools flourished. But generally the public lost interest in twinning when normal channels for cooperation opened up.

In the Netherlands, East–West twinnings have expanded dramatically over the previous decade – from a handful before 1980 to 25 in 1988. Today, Dutch cities have 276 twinnings with the East, 15 of which are with cities in the former Soviet Union. Dutch participants in these linkings initially worked with unofficial groups and political dissidents. Now that many of these contacts are in power, Dutch twinnings are helping them develop civil society and move through the democratization process.

At the first European Conference on East–West Municipal Twinning, held in May 1990 in Rotterdam, 450 delegates from 250 municipalities issued a "challenge" calling for city-to-city measures to strengthen tolerance, peace, justice, and participatory democracy throughout Europe. This declaration reflected the frustration "civil society activists" felt as East–West twinnings became increasingly dominated by "technical issues," such as finance, trade, and foreign investment. A case in point: in 1991 the Dutch provided training for 150 officials and civil servants from Poland, Hungary, and Czechoslovakia, but at the same time, according to Dion van den Berg of the Dutch Interchurch

Peace Council, "there are hardly any contacts being established between local branches of trade unions, peace movements, women's groups, or even local branches of political parties." One reason for this is that local governments treat East–West ties like the old jumelages and fill them with official contacts, sports and cultural exchanges, and educational programs. At the same time civil-society activists have not been able to present sufficiently attractive and specific models of working with other groups in the partner community. The dangers of these trends, says Kees Bode, municipal officer of the city of Rotterdam, can be summarized "in three key words: technocracy, bureaucracy, and centralism – the three enemies of democratic government."

Bode argues:

[A]id programs directed at regional and local government should not only concentrate on the solution of technical problems – although that can be very important – but should also pay substantial attention to the democratization of government itself and procedures used in decision making and execution by regional and local government. Next to that it is important that assistance be given to social groups that are active in democratizing society. At present one should look especially to those groups fighting racism, the enemies of democratization…as well as to groups active in the creation of a society with equal rights and protection of civil rights.

A number of Dutch cities have taken up this challenge. Zaanstad is assisting its twin city of Zwickau, formerly in East Germany, with new programs to help the unemployed. The twinning between Heerlen and Gyor in Hungary is facilitating cooperation between community organizations that serve the elderly. The cities of Nijmegen and Groningen, both twinned with Russian cities (respectively Pskov and Murmansk), are encouraging cooperative projects between organizations of handicapped people. Voorburg created a foundation to oversee its programs in the Czech Republic to improve the position of Gypsies living in Hranice. The Hague and Warsaw are preparing a seminar on the obstacles and achievements in the process of democratization. Twelve Dutch municipalities joined with their Eastern partners to convene an international youth conference in Eindhoven on "Europe's Future – A Common Responsibility: Fighting Racism and Nationalism."

There is growing awareness of the need to widen the scope of twinning schemes to include democratization and justice as municipalities in the East confront worsening economic, social, and political problems. The mayor of one Dutch city, twinned with a Slovakian city with a large Hungarian population, recently said, "Perhaps we should leave our sportsmen…at home for a while, and start concentrating together with our friends and partners in Central and Eastern Europe on the satanic consequences citizens face in the rise of nationalist movements."

Out of these East–West links emerged an unprecedented effort in November 1991 by mayors and other municipal representatives from Europe to help local

THE LIBRARY
U.A.M. DRAWER 3599
MONTICELLO, ARKANSAS 71656

officials from the Yugoslavian republics resolve their ongoing civil war. Organized by the Network for Municipal Peace Policy of the Association of Netherlands Municipalities and the Dutch Interchurch Peace Council, this conference issued a declaration calling on each of the republics to allow individuals to organize anti-war activities. Subsequent conferences were held in Subotica (Serbia), Ohrid (Macedonia), Strasbourg, and many other places. Working closely with the participants in these conferences, the Standing Conference of Local and Regional Authorities of Europe (which is part of the Council of Europe) set up a special committee to monitor the treatment of pro-democracy activists in the cities of the former Yugoslavia.

South–South Relations

The Third World Conference, held in Penang in 1984, declared:

> [T]he industrial countries still want to maintain their stranglehold over commodities, trade, industry, and services. What is now urgently required is a genuine dialogue among concerned people and people's organizations, South–South as well as North–North. And this dialogue must lead to concrete and effective action.

The Penang declaration reflected the frustration and hope felt by many in the South. The frustration is over the imbalances in North–South relations: the rampant exploitation by Northern multinational corporations; the cultural domination by Northern television shows and religions; the counterproductivity of many Northern "development" policies such World Bank projects and IMF structural adjustment; and the Northern assault on the Non-Aligned Movement and the New International Economic Order. As Seydou Sall writes in his Towns and Development report on South–South relations: "Colonialism's worst crime was to undermine the self-confidence of otherwise robust and dignified people, and make them believe that somehow western culture, western religion, western values, western thought models, western technology are superior to their own."

These same Southerners are hopeful, however, that they can delink their economic fate from Northern control and build an alternative economic system in the South that emphasizes grassroots participation and the "informal sector." "In the Zambezi Valley," argues Sall, "the peasants are discovering their own knowledge systems based on a deeper understanding of their culture, their history, their ecology, their belief systems, their spirituality, their values based on fraternity and solidarity, their trees, bushes and seeds." By valuing, storing, and sharing this indigenous knowledge, people in the South can help each other become more self-reliant, both ideologically and financially.

A number of NGOs began promoting this concept of South–South cooperation after the UN Special Session on the African Crisis in 1986. To facilitate

South–South relations and trade, African NGOs established the Forum of Voluntary Development Agencies (FAVDO) in Dakar, and African and Asian NGOs established a South–South Solidarity Network, headquartered in New Delhi. The latter group, according to its organizers, "evolved out of the realization that much of the information on development technologies depends on its availability from Northern development agencies or on information generated in the North."

At one of the North–South NGO Encounters that took place at Cotonou in January 1991, the Southerners participating encouraged Northern NGOs to support South–South networking. The Commonwealth Secretariat, Christian Aid, and Oxfam-UK had actually done this the previous year when they helped underwrite the Bulawayo Conference on South–North Linking for Development to facilitate cooperation among Africans involved in twinning.

•   •   •

In each of these six success stories a relatively small number of communities were able to exert a surprising degree of influence over international affairs. Skeptics try to dismiss these movements by pointing out that, compared to the universe of several hundred thousand communities worldwide, they are inconsequentially small; the anti-nuclear and anti-apartheid movements never involved even 1 percent of the world's communities. Yet *because* most communities are silent, a few speaking out were able to command global attention. The history of CDIs suggests that a hundred or a dozen cities, or even just one bold village, can take leadership on a development issue and set off political tremors across the planet.

CHAPTER 4

Origins

Several factors explain the rise of CDIs. Developments in technology, economics, and politics have created conditions for CDIs to arise in every nation (though these conditions are not equally present from country to country). Country-specific factors suggest why CDIs have been more prevalent in some places than in others. Finally, many communities have come to recognize that they can function effectively at the local level only by acting effectively internationally.

Global Factors

It is commonly said that "the world is shrinking," that "international affairs have become local affairs," that people should "think globally, act locally." Underlying these observations are four conditions that are recent and unique in human history, and that are inescapably part of the landscape of every country.

The first is the growing penetration of global problems. Not long ago a nation and the communities inside it could isolate themselves from international affairs. But an increasing number of problems in one part of the world now have global repercussions. As more countries acquire nuclear, chemical, or biological weapons and mount them atop missiles capable of traveling hundreds or even thousands of miles, there is a greater chance that an isolated conflict will escalate into a regional or global conflagration. No nation can escape the world's environmental problems; ozone depletion, acid rain, and global warming do not respect national boundaries. Nor can nations remove themselves from the powerful forces of the global economy. Within a day a stock market drop in Tokyo can precipitate a financial landslide in Europe and the United States. A war, famine, depression, or natural disaster in one part of the world can send millions of refugees fleeing to another.

A second condition of life in the 1990s is that more and more citizens now have the means to participate in international affairs. Two hundred years ago travel between the continents could be a tumultuous ocean journey of several weeks; now the same distance can be traversed by jet in a matter of hours. A crude message used to move no faster than a letter carried in the pouch of a pony express; now people can send electronic mail, fax documents, or make telephone calls to virtually any part of the world instantly.

The technological revolutions for transportation and communication have several important implications. Authoritarian leaders are finding it increasingly difficult to hide their human-rights abuses or to shield their people from the influence of foreign products, ideas, or visitors. At the same time citizens in all states are finding it easier to connect, meet, and work with counterparts throughout the world. Millions of people now have the basic powers of international travel and discourse that were once held exclusively by a handful of diplomats. With these instruments, citizens have a greater awareness of international problems and a greater commitment to do something about them.

A third, related trend has been the triumph of democracy over totalitarian rule in Eastern Europe and the former Soviet Union and over authoritarian rule in most of Latin America and parts of Africa. For the first time in human history nearly a majority of people have the right to choose their own governments. Repressive systems are becoming obsolete, in part because they can no longer provide for the welfare of their people. The heavy hand of state control inevitably stifles technological innovation and the incentive to work. Violation of human rights leads to international censure and economic deterioration. And once people taste democracy, they do not easily yield power to a military junta or to a rigid party.

This does not mean that the oldest democracies of Europe and North America represent the "end of history," as one US State Department official recently argued, because even "mature" democracies need major overhauls. Every democracy, for example, needs to democratize its secretive, authoritarian structures for making foreign policy. And the growth of powerful regional and global institutions with weak mechanisms for citizen participation – the Council of Europe, the General Agreement on Tariffs and Trade (GATT), and the World Bank are just three of the most obvious examples – poses new threats to democracy. But repression is clearly becoming more costly and precarious for the world's remaining dictators.

The rise of democracy means that hundreds of millions of citizens who were once silenced now have the freedom to speak out, to travel, and to participate in international affairs. Democracy also facilitates the formation of NGOs and local authorities – the main agents of CDIs. After Argentina and the Philippines overthrew their military dictatorships in the 1980s, for example, NGOs and community groups in the two countries multiplied dramatically.

A final trend has been the growing importance of community. As the world becomes more complicated, people are increasingly solving problems at the local level. Community empowerment, of course, is not always positive, because it can serve as a cover for parochialism, tribalism, and racism. But community is also the place we call home. It is where we work and play, where we make friends, where we raise children. It is where political institutions are most accessible and where we can find the resources, legitimacy, and machinery for collective action. A community is a trampoline on which citizens can bounce, gain momentum, and leap into international affairs with far greater force than they ever would have on their own.

These trends help explain why citizens have taken initiatives on so many different global issues: East–West disarmament, Yugoslavian conflict resolution, human rights in South Africa, environmental protection, and, of course, North–South development cooperation. The growing impact of international problems and the expanding opportunities of the global marketplace have given citizens the incentive to participate in world affairs, the declining costs of transportation and communication and the spread of democracy have provided the means, and the rising importance of community has created a political base. The world has changed in ways that have made CDIs inevitable.

Country-specific Factors

CDIs have gathered strength not only because of general global trends but also because of special factors in certain countries. In Belgium, the Netherlands, and the United Kingdom, a key influence was the history of colonialism. Economic and cultural ties to the old colonies, large immigrant populations, and a sense of responsibility about past exploitation of the South have all been key motivations for these nations to initiate CDIs.

Even in Northern countries which never had colonies per se but did have far-reaching foreign-policy "interests," large immigrant populations have lobbied for certain CDIs. In the United States, African Americans were responsible for the sanctions movement against South Africa and Hispanic Americans pressed for solidarity ties with Nicaragua and El Salvador.

The nations of the South, perceiving themselves the victims of colonialism and imperialism, see CDIs as a way of rectifying past injustices. Through linking, for example, Southerners can secure aid, change attitudes in the North, prevent Northern military interventions, cut off Northern support for apartheid, and apply pressure on Northern politicians to restructure the global economy.

A factor related to colonialism is language. UK communities have linked up primarily with Anglophone countries in Africa, Spanish communities with Latin America, and French communities with Francophone Africa.

Two phenomena have been responsible for Europe being the cradle for many CDIs. The first is the post-war process of political and economic integration. This process began with Franco–German reconciliation, which was cemented by French and West German communities setting up more than a thousand jumalages with one another. The development of the European Economic Community further tightened links between European communities as partners in culture, trade, finance, and regional development. To the extent that similar integration processes are beginning in Africa and Latin America, they too will draw communities into regional and international affairs.

Another process that has put global development squarely on the agenda of European cities is mass migration from the East and the South. Gioia Maestro from Italy writes:

> The increase in non-European immigrants in towns is stimulating almost everywhere a discussion on what to do, beyond the administrative measures, to stop this flight from the poorest areas of the world. In this debate the will to define a more coherent and more democratic policy of management of aid to development comes in.

Of course, the reactions of extremists to immigrants, and the concomitant rise of racism and right-wing parties, also raises the urgency for European city councils to articulate more humane policies. Migration also draws Southern communities into international affairs. To many Southerners, the treatment of friends and family members who have moved north is of enormous importance and South–North linking is a simple, powerful tool for expressing solidarity.

Sometimes national suppression of local initiatives has been a catalyst for CDIs. In 1969, when the General Assembly of the United Nations proclaimed "the Second Decade of Development" and called for widespread public education on the issue, several Dutch towns agreed to send money to projects in the South. The Dutch provincial executives and the minister of internal affairs vetoed these CDIs. The president of the Association of Netherlands Municipalities countered that the national government would be unable to influence public opinion on development issues unless it enlisted the support of the political units closest to the people. The debate spread to Parliament and by 1972 the minister of internal affairs decided to allow CDIs. Since this initial struggle, CDIs in the Netherlands have spread rapidly.

Another reason for the emergence of CDIs in some countries is the way in which communities identify with other communities. Drawn to a town with a similar name, Palo Alto, California, became a sister city with Palo in the Philippines. Twinning relationships also may be based on similar city sizes, similar industries, and similar geographic characteristics.

Then, of course, there are special individuals. Behind every CDI lies one or more leaders. Sometimes they are national politicians, local officials, or party chairs who are seeking to embrace a popular cause. Sometimes they are NGO leaders, missionaries, consultants, or charismatic citizens who are committed to the issues of peace, justice, or ecology. The link between Murzzuschlag, Austria, and Arusha, Tanzania, began when an Austrian student won a radio-announcing competition and called for a greater national commitment to the South. Norbert Noisser writes about Germany: "In most of the cases, especially in smaller or medium-sized municipalities, local authorities or the mayor have been confronted with North-South issues through the initiative of active local citizens. In these cases, the personal engagement of individuals is decisive."

Community Motivations

Closely related to the question of how CDIs originate is what motivates communities to undertake them. Part of the answer is suggested by the discussion in Chapter 1 of the myriad ways CDIs genuinely promote people-centered development. CDIs help empower people in the South and the North, they cut gigantic international problems down to a manageable size, they put local expertise to good use, and they provide more opportunities for action than national governments do.

But what is really in it for communities? Why are CDIs in *their* interest? Existing evidence suggests that CDIs enable members of a community to achieve six important goals: to become part of a shrinking world, to act on feelings of global responsibility and solidarity, to lower the local costs of global problems, to secure the economic advantages of global relationships, to enjoy the benefits of cultural exchanges, and to increase local political participation.

Becoming Part of Global Society

A central goal for human beings everywhere is dignity. In a shrinking world, people are searching for recognition not only from their friends, neighbors, and countrymen but also from the international community. CDIs provide people with practical means to recognize, and to be recognized by, others thousands of miles away.

In his paper on "South–North Linking: A Southern Perspective," Peter Nyoni writes: "The noble ideals of international understanding, of cross cultural understanding, of unity and peace in international and interpersonal relations account for much in the motivation for community linking in both South and North."

Many communities in the South have embraced CDIs because they empower Southerners to speak in their own voices. Moussa Conteh sees CDIs as a way to overcome the legacy of colonialism. He notes: "We have to start the slow but rewarding search for our identity, establish our presence and regain our confidence. Our very presence was denied by our colonial masters, and if for some reason notice was taken of it, our very humanity was questioned."

CDIs give Southerners a new opportunity to assert themselves and to establish new, more equal relationships with Northerners. "Once people develop a sense of their own identity and value," argues Conteh, "they can become valuable agents of change."

Certainly this is true for Northerners as well. CDIs give them the opportunity to shed the dehumanizing role of colonial master. By enabling Northerners to come to grips with their past and to experience international relationships rooted in mutual respect, CDIs facilitate basic human evolution.

Meeting Global Responsibilities

A second common reason why citizens in communities start CDIs is to act on their feelings of global responsibility. In Northern Europe, where people have a strong social tradition of helping the less fortunate, CDIs are viewed as part of each individual's obligation to humanity. Tor Henrik Andersen of Norway writes: "In the Nordic countries...our cultural heritage and our sense of values have often been the reason for becoming involved in the first place." Paul van Tongeren of the Netherlands reports that "our society and culture, which treasure values such as human rights, liberty, democracy, and Christian and human-itarian traditions, oblige all of us, including local authorities, to be involved and show commitment to solving major global problems."

Almost every country has some tradition of helping others in need. This sense of duty is most plainly visible when cities come to the aid of victims of a disaster. After a major earthquake hit the Armenian cities of Leninakan, Spitak, and Kirovakan in December 1988, killing 25,000 people and injuring tens of thousands of others, US–Soviet sister-city committees spontaneously kicked into action. Dr Roy Farrell, an emergency-room surgeon fluent in Russian and a veteran participant in Seattle's sister-city program with Tashkent, was one of the first to decide to go. Within three days Dr Farrell assembled hundreds of thousands of dollars' worth of medical supplies from local hospitals, cooking and camping equipment from Recreational Equipment, Inc., a Boeing 747 jet from Flying Tigers, and a team of 30 other Americans, including 13 physicians and twelve paramedics. Working alongside other charitable organizations, US sister-city groups delivered millions of dollars of food, blankets, and building materials to the demolished areas.

Even communities with limited economic endowments want to help fellow human beings who are in need. The city of Dushanbe in the former Soviet Union provided $200,000 of clothes, blankets, shoes, and other assistance to people living in Lusaka, Dushanbe's twin in Zambia, when floods hit in 1989. Lusaka returned the favor in 1990 when it responded to food shortages in Dushanbe by sending packed consignments of corn, potatoes, avocados, and pineapples.

Many communities wish not only to provide charitable contributions but also want to right fundamental wrongs. Following the motto of Towns and Devel-opment – "From charity to justice" – these localities seek to eliminate the economic, political, and social injustices facing most of the world's people. Sometimes the word used to describe the underlying emotion people feel when fighting injustice is "solidarity." Solidarity occurs when a person stands side by side with those experiencing oppression and joins their struggle to resist that oppression. A good example of solidarity, detailed in the next section, is the network of 400 American and European communities that linked up with Nicaragua throughout the 1980s, when the United States was trying to oust the

Sandinista government by applying economic sanctions and by arming the contra rebels.

Reducing the Local Costs of International Problems

For many communities the fallout from underdevelopment is no longer abstract. Consider some of the specific costs American communities face because of poverty in Central and South America. Tired of low wages, repression, and war, millions of Latin Americans have illegally entered the United States, stretching the social services of thousands of communities and driving down wages throughout the country. Because poor farmers in the Andes find coca a profitable crop to grow, and because the debt-ridden countries of Colombia, Peru, and Bolivia cannot afford to shut down the drug lords, imports of crack cocaine into the United States have steadily increased and turned its streets into war zones. (In Washington, DC, a city of 600,000 people, nearly 500 died of handgun murders in 1991, mostly in connection with drug trafficking.)

Poverty in one part of the world is increasingly harming communities everywhere. Jobs in wealthy countries are lost as multinational companies cross boundaries to take advantage of sub-subsistence wages. Jobs in poor countries are not created because impoverished consumers lack the income to purchase the products manufactured by mobile companies. With the threats of ozone depletion and global warming looming large, summer resorts face the prospect that people may no longer be able to swim or to tan outdoors, coastal communities shudder about being inundated by rising ocean levels (unless they build expensive dikes), and agricultural communities worry about becoming dust bowls. Impoverished countries also are breeding grounds for demagogues and pariahs who may seek to increase their prestige by acquiring nuclear, chemical, and biological weapons – and perhaps by using them.

No locality can eliminate these problems by acting alone. Nevertheless, a number of communities have gone beyond those who say NIMBY ("not in my backyard") and have begun practicing a new philosophy called BIMBY, "*begin* in my backyard." They are recognizing that by setting an example of good global citizenship, they can persuade other communities to join them. Thus, a growing number of cities are outlawing chlorofluorocarbons and other ozone-depleting chemicals and requiring reductions in carbon-dioxide emissions, not because these programs produce economic benefits (few do in the short term), but because these policies are necessary for planetary survival.

Securing Economic Benefits from International Relations

For some communities, CDIs hold the lure of economic gain. The economic motive certainly is key for Southern communities that hope to use CDIs to acquire aid, technology, loans, or know-how for their own economic development. (Most Southern twinning partners, however, consider the quality of their relationships with the North at least as important as the net proceeds.)

In striking contrast to most European twinning programs, 80 percent of the US communities twinned with localities in the South and affiliated with Sister Cities International are involved in business promotion. US mayors frequently travel to the South to attract foreign investment or to hawk products made by local companies. For example, Mayor David Dinkins of New York said that one objective of his recent trip to South Africa was to establish markets for the products and services of New York companies once a majority government comes to power in Pretoria. It should be noted that rarely is the motive purely self-interest, for the practitioners of neoliberal trade policy believe in the theory of "comparative advantage," that economic benefits accrue to both sellers and buyers.

The motive of economic self-interest is more transparent in Japan, where cities have tried to use CDIs to spruce up their "city/prefectural image" for business and tourist purposes. In some instances Japanese chambers of commerce have used "technical assistance" programs as a way to bring unskilled laborers into the country. This example suggests how well-intentioned economic behavior, if not rooted in truly equal partnerships, can lead to exploitation.

Gaining Cultural Enrichment

The two most common CDIs – development education and twinning – enrich local cultural life. Throughout the world one hears effusive descriptions of people-to-people exchanges, pen-pal relationships, art shows, festivals, concerts, bazaars, and hundreds of other activities that make communities with CDIs more exciting places to live.

In Europe development education and twinning are also viewed as enhancing tolerance, understanding, and empathy for foreigners within the community. The recent surge of attacks on refugees has underscored the need to find better ways to integrate foreign visitors, guest workers, and refugees into localities. Tor Henrik Andersen of Norway writes:

> Links challenge our normal way of thinking and our prejudices. They help us…to counteract racist tendencies, acting as a mirror to our own society and own lifestyles. They help to give *the others* a face, so that it becomes more and more difficult for *us* to live at *their* expense.

Increasing Political Participation

A sixth benefit of CDIs for communities is enhanced political participation. CDIs generate popular interest and excitement, and they open up opportunities for concerned citizens to participate in international affairs. One of the highest turnouts ever recorded at a city council meeting in Palo Alto, California, occurred when the local legislators debated a resolution supporting "a bilateral, verifiable freeze of the nuclear arms race."

The provision of grants to various groups using CDIs also can enhance political participation. The city of Derry in Ireland found that its annual grant of £2,000 ($3,600) to the local Development Education Centre (DEC) was a worthy investment when the DEC coordinated a massive campaign to prevent Dupont from building a gigantic waste incinerator. The campaign included 62 community groups and ultimately a majority of the city council. Had the city not supported CDIs, it might have well ended up with an unwanted incinerator and greater citizen distrust of municipal government.

Finally, CDIs can strengthen civil society. They create bridges of cooperation between citizens and elected officials on issues of increasing importance worldwide. They represent participatory democracy at its best.

• • •

All these factors suggest that CDIs are hardly a passing fad. They are an inevitable manifestation of a shrinking world. Even though communities in some countries have been drawn into the CDI movement faster than others, sooner or later communities in every country will probably get involved. The reason is simple: CDIs enable communities to solve practical local problems and become better places to live. But not all players on the international stage see these changes in such positive terms.

Responses

The Cologne Appeal was "addressed to local authorities, NGOs, and community groups throughout Europe," but CDIs have reached other audiences as well, including national governments, international organizations, and women. The responses generally have been favorable, though within each of these groups there are skeptics and critics.

NGOs and Community Groups

Many NGOs and community groups entered partnerships with local authorities because the job of global development seemed too big to pursue on their own. They realized that the formal involvement of local government could boost their work with money, legitimacy, coordination, and special skills. Community groups in Germany, for example, saw that by working in a broader coalition with municipalities they could educate the public more effectively; One World Weeks, exhibitions, and cultural events reach more people when they have city sponsorship.

But some NGOs and community groups remain wary of working too closely with local authorities, and some eschew joint action altogether. Participating in a larger coalition can mean losing one's freedom of action. An organization that once was a forceful advocate of, say, fair trade suddenly may find itself part of a watered-down, apolitical campaign for "world harmony." Some German NGOs complain that local governments are inclined to create development policies that are inoffensive, fuzzy, and boring. Japanese NGOs are reluctant to work with municipal bodies because the latter are essentially taking orders from the national government. The same is true throughout much of the South, where, according to Manab Chakraborty of India,

> there is a fair degree of mutual apprehension, if not hostility, between Southern local authorities and popular organizations. Notable exceptions to this are Bulawayo (Zimbabwe), Freetown (Sierra Leone) and Pune (India). The local authorities in the South are seen as part of a centralised bureaucracy, often bankrupt, and devoid of any real power, care, and concern for ordinary citizens.

Some NGOs and community groups fear that local authorities might usurp their work. "It is often the case," writes Shin Yoshida of Japan, "that an innovative NGO starts a new program/project. But after several years of hard work and good outcomes, local government comes in and, not by supporting the NGO, will take over what the NGO has established." NGOs in the Philippines are reluctant to work with local authorities, because starting in the 1950s Filipino local officials carried out "community development" programs with funds from the US Central Intelligence Agency and the US Agency in International Development and thus became closely linked with US covert actions and counterinsurgency activities.

Then there is always the danger of discontinuity when a local government changes political hands. NGOs or community groups may suddenly find their work suspended if an election sweeps local leaders out of office. Some of the Nicaraguan links with the North went defunct after the Sandinistas lost control of the national government and a number of city councils in 1990.

Despite these risks, NGOs and community groups have seen enough virtues in joint action to launch CDIs in practically every country studied. They have protected their freedom of action by working with local authorities provisionally and continuing their independent programs. Joint action also seems to succeed in communities where an advisory forum composed of representatives of key NGOs and community groups can serve as a counterweight to the city council. The village of Patzun in Guatemala, for example, has a "nonpolitical, elected, management committee" that helps oversee its relationship with the Norwegian community of Krakeroy.

Local Authorities

A growing number of local officials are becoming convinced of the value of working with NGOs and community groups. Informal organizations can help them reach more people, draw in a broader range of constituencies, and mobilize larger numbers of volunteers. Nevertheless, not all municipal leaders are sanguine about joint action.

Local governments that are organs of national government or that lack democratic structures are especially loath to open themselves to NGOs and community groups. Eduardo Galeazzi and Juan Luis Merega note that some Argentinian local governments have steered clear of grassroots groups, because local authorities have "an excessively bureaucratized structure (which is unable to solve problems) or an excessively politicized structure (which solves them wrongly, looking for a political advantage)."

NGOs and community groups often claim to be "non-partisan" or "bipartisan," but in fact are very partisan, and local officials must weigh the political consequences of working with one group and not with another. A city that decides to formulate a global warming project by collaborating with ecological organizations but not with corporations may well alienate the business community. Cooperating with firms but not environmentalists could be equally unpopular.

Because politicians are held accountable at the next election, they tend to be more cautious than NGOs and community groups. Some local officials are afraid of associating themselves with groups that propose radical actions or make "irresponsible" remarks. Many German cities ducked CDIs altogether before the 1980s, arguing that global development is a "foreign policy" matter best left to national leaders.

In an era of tightening budgets and worsening urban decay, local officials resist CDIs that require expenditures of money. For example, when 250 Eritrean children arrived in London in the summer of 1990, seven local boroughs refused to take responsibility for them, and other boroughs dragged their feet until legal action was threatened. More generally the relationship between London's NGOs and local authorities on the issue of refugees has seesawed between cooperation and confrontation and demonstrated the resistance of local officials to take on politically explosive issues. UK NGOs and local authorities agree that the central government should take more responsibility but disagree over the appropriate role of local authorities. Some local officials, playing to rising public apprehensions and racism over refugees, seem eager to find any excuse possible to ignore or to expel foreigners.

As international affairs permeate more and more aspects of community life, local politicians will find it increasingly perilous to ignore citizen demands for CDIs. Too many groups with too much clout are insisting upon local action. Officials would rather try to frame these demands in cost-effective and non-polarizing ways than to avoid them altogether. One means they use to depoliticize CDIs is to create special boards in which all political parties are represented. The Norwegian town of Krakeroy, mentioned earlier, relates with Patzun through a friendship committee comprised of five council members – one from each party on the council.

As was true with NGOs and community groups, local officials in every country studied are taking up CDIs. Moreover, organizations of cities like the Association of Netherlands Municipalities, which resisted CDIs a decade ago, now have paid staff working on CDIs and are goading more elected officials to become involved. These precedents make it easier for local governments in other countries to embrace CDIs.

National Governments

National governments have had four different reactions to CDIs: indifference, orchestration, opposition, and cooperation. Perhaps the most common reaction has been indifference. Fifty years ago national governments could not conceive of their communities participating in foreign policy. Even today, the dominant school of thought in international relations theory – *Realpolitik* – regards sub-national actors as largely irrelevant.

Starting in the 1950s, however, a few governments in the North began to recognize that local actions could serve their own national foreign-policy interests. The French and German foreign-policy-makers who implemented Jean Monnet's vision of a unified Coal and Steel Community to prevent another world war in Europe supported the formation of a thousand jumalages between French and German cities. President Dwight Eisenhower began the sister-cities program in the United States as a way of promoting capitalism and democracy through people-to-people exchange. The Dutch government in the 1970s realized that it could not hope to influence public opinion on North–South development strategies if the authorities closest to the people were shut out of the debate. And now the Japanese government is leading a campaign to "internationalize" the country to shore up its power in trade by financing "foreign trainee" programs in 47 prefectures and nine cities.

When municipalities push CDIs beyond a certain point, however, national governments try to regulate them. The Dutch, British, and German national governments all raised questions about whether their local governments had the legal power to spend money abroad. Ultimately national and local authorities in these countries hammered out a compromise in which municipal money could be given to countrymen who were working in the South.

The more that CDIs intruded on the traditional foreign-policy domain of national governments, the stronger the backlash. Thus, in the United States, where many cities have framed their CDIs in terms of "municipal foreign policy," national edicts and court cases have set several significant limits. US cities can divest from firms doing business in South Africa, but they cannot ban nuclear-weapons work by private contractors. Nor can governors prevent their state militia forces from being sent for training abroad.

In the United Kingdom a national attack on CDIs coincided with an all-out war against local government. In the mid-1980s Prime Minister Margaret Thatcher, irritated with progressive community initiatives, abolished a half-dozen city councils, including the Greater London Council, which meant that many local government functions were taken over by the central government (the remainder devolved to 32 weak borough authorities). Thatcher also placed "rate-capping" requirements on UK local governments, forcing them to cut taxes and programs. Rarely regarded as life-or-death matters like food or housing subsidies, CDIs were often the first programs to fall victim to the budget-cutters' knives. One of the early casualties, for example, was Reading's ambitious International Forum, which had financed exhibitions, festivals, arts, and linking programs.

It is worth noting that in both the United States and the United Kingdom controversial CDIs were pursued alongside less partisan CDIs. Nuclear-free zones were creating deep splits in UK public opinion, but development education and linking were more broadly accepted. In the United States, while progressive constituencies were pushing city councils to condemn the arms race, to divest from South Africa, and to link with Nicaragua, more moderate constituencies were promoting sister cities and global trade.

Elsewhere in the North, where national governments have been less conservative, conflict between national and local officials has been kept to a minimum. Indeed, in countries such as Canada, Finland, France, Germany, the Netherlands, Norway, and Zimbabwe, communities pursued their CDIs in close cooperation with national agencies. The leaders of these countries wisely recognized that global development presented too many complex issues to be handled exclusively through their foreign ministries. In some cases, such as Canada, Germany, and the Netherlands, government support included large subsidies for participating local authorities, NGOs, and community groups.

As noted in the previous chapter, communities in countries that are relatively wealthy, democratic, and decentralist have been the most likely to initiate CDIs. This suggests that as other countries become wealthier, more democratic, and more decentralist, CDIs should begin to pass through the same phases that occurred in North America and Europe. It is not surprising that communities in Japan, Italy, Greece, Spain, and much of the South, where decentralization is beginning to occur, are also just beginning to take CDIs seriously. Thus far most CDIs in these countries have been consistent with national policy. But if the pattern exhibited elsewhere in the North holds, more controversial local initiatives may not be far away.

International Organizations

Given the disappointing track record of the World Bank and the IMF in promoting people-centered development, many CDI organizers are loath to work with these global agencies. To those who believe that the Bretton-Woods institutions have caused more poverty and suffering than they have alleviated, even the act of accepting money from them is suspect. Likewise, officials at the World Bank and the IMF, unaccustomed to thinking in figures smaller than a billion dollars, have trouble seeing the importance of CDIs.

Nevertheless, there are some recent instances where international organizations have supported CDIs. The World Bank and Italy, for example, set up a municipal development program for Sub-Saharan Africa in collaboration with the International Union of Local Authorities, the Federation of Canadian Municipalities, and several other organizations of cities. The United Nations Development Program and Habitat also have invested in urban development in Africa.

The international organizations that ultimately may matter most for CDIs are those created for and by local authorities. Falling into this category are the International Council for Local Environmental Initiatives (ICLEI), the United Towns Organisation, and Towns and Development. Regional organizations with mechanisms for local government participation also might be helpful. The Council of Europe and the European Commission, for example, have provided financial support for Towns and Development for seven years.

Women

The Cologne Appeal stressed that development projects must recognize "the significance of women in the development process and [ensure] that projects benefit and enhance the status of women." Why? As a linking partner in Bangladesh observes:

> If you are going to educate a nation, you have to start with the women, because they are the ones who spread that knowledge further. If you teach a man something, he takes his knowledge with him when he goes out to plough his field. But give that knowledge to a woman and she shares it with her whole family, so it reaches a great many more people.

Some CDI practitioners have heeded this advice. Two community groups in Risor, Norway, helped 420 women in the Gambian village of Sutukoba obtain plots of land to grow vegetables. Another linking group in Norway, based in Nesodden, raised 1.2 million kroner ($187,000) through a television show to help educate women living in the poorest villages of Bangladesh. Some of Austria's linking projects in Nicaragua have focused on the development of female farmers. When De Bilt in the Netherlands decided to build a public health center in Gakpe, Benin, it made special efforts to involve women's groups. And Bremen designed some of its biogas digesters to be used primarily by women in Pune, India.

But these examples are exceptional. Most programs exhibit very little fine-tuning for the needs of women. Moreover, there have been very few studies of whether or not CDIs benefit women. This kind of inquiry could lead to some startling discoveries. Dutch CDI organizers recently learned that many of the Southern cooperatives participating in the Max Havelaar "solidarity coffee" campaign excluded women. Subsequent debate led Northern organizers to insist that these cooperatives be opened up to women. This kind of scrutiny is badly needed for all CDIs.

•   •   •

It was perhaps inevitable that the CDI movement would encounter resistance. Like many other social movements, it upsets traditional understandings, modes of thinking, and relationships. It takes power away from one group of players and gives it to another. It threatens to rearrange the ground rules of international affairs.

But CDIs build on powerful global trends. Throughout the world local officials are gradually yielding to NGOs and communities, national officials to communities, and men to women. These changes are proceeding slowly – for many too slowly – but the direction of change is unmistakable. The external obstacles to CDIs are beginning to crumble. The most significant remaining problem may well be the short-sightedness of CDI practitioners themselves.

CHAPTER 6

Challenges for the
Twenty-first Century

Like any political movement, the CDI movement is riddled with weaknesses, mistakes, and contradictions. Unfortunately, the proponents of CDIs – people who are generally optimistic, upbeat, encouraging – tend to downplay or ignore these problems. But a movement can succeed only if it is self-critical. Weaknesses must be addressed, mistakes rectified, and contradictions resolved. A movement that cannot learn, grow, and change will soon become extinct.

This chapter lays out 14 challenges facing CDI practitioners. Each challenge highlights both the difficulties facing cities and potential solutions.

Improving Data

Despite the diligent efforts of many analysts, relatively little is known about CDIs. In 1990 the board of Towns and Development and several outside advisors drew up a proposal to study CDIs. The plan was to bring together 34 leading CDI theorists and practitioners from 18 countries to prepare rigorous reports that would follow carefully designed guidelines and research methods. The estimated price-tag was over $800,000.

Ultimately, less than 5 percent of this budget was raised to prepare a report on CDIs for the Berlin conference. Given the enormous gap between the money needed and the amount spent, it is a testament to the dedication of the writers that the conference received as many interesting and detailed papers as it did. Nevertheless, much of the reporting in these papers was vague and impressionistic.

In most countries even the simplest numbers – how many communities have linking programs, how much money is being spent, how many citizens are involved – are unavailable. Where extensive surveys have been performed, as in Spain and the United States, the responses are relatively few and not always complete.

Two other problems face CDI data-gatherers: terminology and categorization. What is considered sister-city work in one country is called development education in another. Moreover, how should official links be compared with unofficial links? What constitutes official approval?

These problems are especially difficult for analysts in the South, where the absence of roads, telephones, photocopiers, and fax machines hamper the collection of data. Gabriel C. Banda, who prepared a report on CDIs in Zambia, had difficulty finding information about twinning ties abroad. The Zambian government kept poor records, and foreign embassies and diplomatic missions knew little about what their local governments were doing. Even when Banda was able to find national and local information about twinning, the two sources sometimes contradicted each other (e.g., concerning the dates of certain twinning arrangements).

The difficulties facing analysts who prepared issue reports from the Berlin conference were also formidable. Without a budget for travel and international telephone interviews, they could not easily identify the key players in other countries. Most countries do not have a single knowledgeable person who possesses information about, say, environmental CDIs. A country may have ten key people, each working on one environmental issue, with no one knowing the entire field. Getting information from ten people 5,000 miles away is tough, especially if those people are competitive with each other. The basic problem is that, for most issues, coherent national networks are in their infancy and global networks simply do not exist.

Even if a researcher could count exactly the number of Nicaraguan twinnings or South African divestment policies, she still would not know much about them. How many volunteers participated in these programs? How many local officials? How much money did they spend annually? The list of interesting questions is endless.

Right now, the answers to these questions are spotty, except in a handful of countries like the Netherlands or the United States where data collection has been going on for years. Without data, measuring the political importance of CDIs is difficult, if not impossible.

The first challenge for the CDI movement, therefore, is to find an individual, an NGO, or a local authority within each country who is willing to serve as a national point person to collect, update, and improve key data on CDIs on a regular basis. To help motivate national point people to gather data, Towns and Development or another organization might consider publishing each year a compendium of CDI data from around the world.

Making Hard-headed Evaluations

One consequence of weak data is that serious evaluation of CDIs is exceedingly rare. For many of those writing about CDIs, personal feelings often comprise the entirety of evaluation. In the report from Norway, for example, the linkage between Suldal and the Nepali villages of Urma and Urmi was examined in the following terms: "The villagers celebrated [the Norwegians' visit] with music and dancing. They very much appreciated having friends visit them." The underlying logic is that if either Northern or Southern partners are dissatisfied, they simply will stop participating and the link will be dissolved.

Certainly continued commitment on both sides is one important test for whether a North–South relationship is mutually beneficial, but it is not the only one. A more serious evaluation of Suldal's link with Urma and Urmi might ask the following questions: What were the short- and long-term impacts of Suldal's visit? Who benefited? Who lost? Was there really joint planning and consultation? Was there genuine human growth on both sides? Did the visit equip both communities to be more responsible participants in world affairs?

At the November 1990 conference on South–North Linking for Development held in Bulawayo, Zimbabwe, Southern participants were incensed about Northern behavior in linking. Some were angry that Northern groups were using negative stereotypes of Africa, such as pictures of starving children, for fundraising. Others were frustrated that aid packages sometimes contained medications that had expired. A few felt that their Northern partners assumed they knew the needs of the South without even asking.

Unfortunately, voicing general concerns at a conference is no substitute for giving ongoing, specific criticism. Northern CDI partners seem too willing to assume that the enthusiasm of their Southern partners (or their silence) means that CDIs are working, while Southern partners seem too eager to criticize the North in general terms rather than risk offending the practitioners who implement inappropriate CDIs.

Another problem with evaluation is that the sheer number of CDIs is taken to be an indicator of success. But quantity does not mean quality. In the United States more than 700 North–South sister-city relationships exist on paper, but many, perhaps most, are defunct. The Dutch regard the steady increase in the number of their linkings as a sign that CDIs are advancing, while the Finns conclude that the absence of a growing number of CDIs means that its movement is weakening. In fact these numbers say very little. A dramatic increase in linking, especially where a given community is taking on more partners abroad, can be a sign of superficiality, and a slow-down might indicate a period of deepening and maturing.

Northerners and Southerners should come together to prepare guidelines for evaluating CDIs and disseminate them widely. Moreover, they should carry out evaluations together. Northern and Southern communities can use joint evaluation as an opportunity to listen to and learn from one another.

Connecting Development Education to Political Action

At first glance, it is hard to criticize any development education program. Who can find fault with a process that is motivating people to absorb new informa-

tion, to learn new skills, to translate new knowledge into action? Certainly any class, event, booklet, film, or activity that accomplishes these goals is a positive step forward. Yet if development education is a process in which we ask questions, then tough questions must be asked of it.

How well is development education imparting new information to people? Classes are occurring, events are being held, films are being shown, but there is no hard evidence that people are really learning and maturing.

The 11.11.11 Campaign in Belgium is a good example of an educational program that actually may be teaching very little. Critics of the campaign say it has been more successful at fund-raising than educating. Of course, there is nothing wrong with "Third World markets," festivals, or guerrilla theater, but do these activities convey important pieces of information about North–South relations? Does Salsa music help people understand the debt predicament of Latin America? Do traditional crafts from Kenya heighten awareness of President Daniel arap Moi's human-rights abuses?

If development education were really working, why are the countries of the North so reluctant to cancel even part of the South's debt or to share a paltry 0.7 percent of their national income? One might reply that without development education official policies would be much worse. But if the goal of development education is to stimulate action and change, it has clearly not succeeded.

Practitioners of development education must strive to pass on more than information; they must motivate people to ask tough questions about development policies (including policies advocated by development education specialists) and they must push people to become politically engaged. One effective means of doing the latter is to connect global issues to very specific community and personal actions. Public education campaigns advocating lifestyle change, for example, such as those associated with the Green Municipalities program in Denmark, seem to be having some impact. It also may be essential to adopt the teaching methods advocated by Paolo Freire in *Pedagogy of the Oppressed*, in which learning and political empowerment go hand in hand. Finally, Northerners and Southerners should come together to exchange their experiences with development education.

Greening CDIs

The total level of economic activity in the world has already exceeded the ecological carrying capacity of the planet. The ozone layer is thinning, the global climate is warming, fertile soils are being exhausted, and species are disappearing by the thousands. Business cannot continue as usual.

Further economic development threatens to exacerbate these looming environmental problems in two ways. As long as underdevelopment continues, the

world's one billion poorest people will cut down forests for firewood, reproduce at an accelerating rate, and dump human wastes and sewage into lakes and rivers without treatment. Continued overdevelopment will lead the world's one billion richest people to exhaust the earth's supplies of food, water, biomass, and energy by eating too much meat, by driving gas-guzzling cars, and by generating huge quantities of solid and toxic wastes. For example, compared with the Japanese (who themselves are overconsumers), Americans use 2.5 times as much energy and produce twice as much garbage per capita.

Development analyst David Korten notes:

> In between the overconsumers and the marginals are 3 billion sustainers who travel by bicycle and public transportation; eat healthy diets of grains and vegetables supplemented by small amounts of meat; drink clean, unbottled water; and recycle most of their wastes. They live in basic harmony with the earth's ecology.

To protect the environment and to ensure the long-term survival of humanity, CDIs must accomplish two missions: they must raise the standard of living of the world's poor, and they must change the lifestyles of the rich.

To help the poor, the precepts of people-centered development suggest that communities should transfer skills instead of aid and should strive to make the world economy more just. But sustainable development also requires the transfer of environmentally benign technology. With the right tools, the South can develop in a way that leapfrogs over the North's ecological mistakes. Why build super-highways for cars when you can spend the same money on efficient mass transit? Why construct energy-wasteful buildings when passive-solar designs are available? Why install incandescent lightbulbs in a new house when highly efficient compact fluorescents last longer and have a lower lifetime cost? Communities in both the North and South can play a leading role in developing, producing, and distributing these kinds of appropriate technologies. "since in Third World cities physical infrastructure may reach only one-third to half of the population," writes Janice Perlman, director of the Megacities Project, "there is a great opportunity to skip over the wasteful and capital-intensive technologies of the past and move over right to 21st century solutions."

The Cologne Appeal emphasized the importance of lifestyle change, particularly in the North. In the seven years since the appeal was first issued it has become obvious that elites in both the North and the South will have to reduce their consumption. Unfortunately, few communities are taking this goal very seriously. Only a minority of communities with CDIs seem to be raising awareness about the inefficient use of energy or water, the failure to recycle scarce materials, the overuse of automobiles, and the unnecessary consumption of beef. And most of these forward-looking communities do not have comprehensive programs for promoting energy conservation, recycling, mass transit, or

more healthful diets. CDIs in the future must push more aggressively for lifestyle changes in both the North and the South.

The question whether technological fixes alone, without lifestyle change, can allow future inhabitants of the planet to live sustainably is unanswerable and irrelevant. Global environmental crises today are so urgent that communities must implement both agendas as vigorously as possible.

CDIs to improve the environment are among the simplest and most effective actions that a Northern and Southern community can undertake in partnership with one another. A creative example is the Climate Alliance, in which Northern communities cut energy use while Southern NGOs protect tropical rainforests. The city of Breda in the Netherlands went a step further and designed a joint action plan to combat global warming. Breda planted a forest near a local highway to compensate for carbon-dioxide emissions, while helping its Polish sister city plant another forest and co-financing a forestry association in Botswana.

Once Northern and Southern partners are working together on environmental problems, they can begin to address some troubling questions raised by CDIs. Are development-education materials worth the forests that had to be cut to manufacture them? Is all the jet fuel consumed and high-altitude pollution produced when a Northerner flies south worth the benefits of linking? Is the Finnish city of Tampere acting wisely when it cuts down and sells Christmas trees to finance reforestation projects in Mwanza, Tanzania?

Addressing Issues of Global Political Economy

If the Cologne Appeal's slogan – "From charity to justice" – is ever to be realized, CDIs will have to address two fundamental issues concerning North–South economic relations: the $1.3 trillion debt the South owes to the North, and the unfair structure of world trade.

The debt crisis began in the 1970s, when Northern bankers, eager to recycle tens of billions of dollars of new deposits from wealthy oil-producing nations, talked Southern leaders into taking massive development loans. Northern economists, including those in the World Bank, sold the South on the false promise that gigantic projects, such as hydroelectric dams in the Amazon jungle, could lead the way to rapid industrialization. Some Northerners also lobbied Southern leaders to use these loans to buy state-of-the-art weapons from the North. Most Southern leaders took the loans with no popular mandate, and not a few lined their pockets while the great majority of their countrymen lived in destitution.

Just about the only individuals not responsible for the debt crisis are those who are now paying most dearly for it: poor people in the South. The structural adjustment programs of the World Bank and the IMF have forced Southern countries to devalue their currencies, to slash public sector jobs, and to cut subsidies for food, housing, health care, and education. The result has been increasing

poverty. At the same time Northern efforts to protect their own markets and to scuttle global commodity agreements have made it impossible for the South to trade its way out of debt.

Some Northerners propose debt-for-nature swaps as an answer. But the fact is that the 25 swaps arranged thus far have had a trivial impact on the $1.4 trillion debt. Moreover, these swaps are controversial because they surrender national sovereignty over valuable lands. In some instances control of the land was ceded to foreigners without ever consulting the indigenous peoples living there. Debt-for-nature swaps may protect a few forests, but they do little to improve the overall fairness of North–South economic relations.

Until the South's debts are forgiven or otherwise canceled, the nations of the South will have to export more than they import to earn foreign exchange. This will mean continued austerity and social suffering, increased burdens on the environment, and no prospect for self-reliance. As the Peruvian economist Jagvier Iguiniz notes: "I do not like Western solutions to the debt crisis – they kill too many people."

A second problem facing the global economy is chimera of "free trade." When economist David Ricardo argued in 1817 that free trade would benefit every nation because of the law of comparative advantage, he assumed that capital was immobile. Today, however, multinational corporations move freely around the globe, essentially unaccountable to any nation, in search of low wages and cheap resources. Every country – indeed, every community in every country – is now competing for corporate investment. To make themselves "competitive," governments seek to cut wages and benefits, to ease environmental standards, and to remove product safety laws. A frenzied competition is now at work, "harmonizing" downward nations' standards for workers, consumers, and the environment. If current trends continue, the level of corporate exploitation now rife in the South will soon be seen worldwide.

Downward harmonization of environmental standards poses especially serious risks. In the few years since the ominous Brundtland report, there is new evidence that global environmental problems are worse than predicted. The ozone layer is being destroyed faster than expected; people, animals, and plants living in the middle latitudes may soon experience the dangers of exposure to higher doses of ultraviolet radiation. Over the next few decades some global warming appears all but certain, which will mean melting icecaps, rising ocean levels, coastal flooding, and spreading deserts. Ocean pollution has become so pronounced that it is becoming difficult to purchase fish that are not laced with unhealthful levels of mercury, PCBs, or other poisons.

The rules of the game for trade allow companies to move freely across boundaries but not workers, provide no minimum standards for labor rights or environmental protection, and remove from local governments important freedoms to regulate, to invest, or to enter contracts as they see fit. Until the fairness of global trade is improved, perhaps by putting a social charter in GATT

analogous to that binding on the countries of the European Community, a growing number of Northern firms will continue old patterns of exploitation by setting up sweatshops in the South.

Few communities in either the North or the South are discussing these global problems and hardly any are designing CDIs to solve them. To be sure, communities cannot easily address these issues, but nevertheless they have options: they can raise public awareness about the debt crisis and fair trade; they can lobby national officials and international organizations to cancel debts and to add a social charter to GATT; they can begin working together with other communities internationally to grade the behavior of corporations and to apply sanctions against the biggest offenders. If even ten percent of the world's cities were to refuse buying products from or investing in the stocks and bonds of irresponsible companies, the behavior of many firms might change. In the United States it took the divestment of only a small percentage of state and local funds to convince two-thirds of US companies with equity ties in South Africa to stop doing business with Pretoria.

The view of most Southern CDI partners is that Northern communities must make these issues central to their development activities. If a Northern community sends millions of dollars'-worth of aid and technology to its sister city in Brazil, and yet at the same time supports national politicians who refuse to relieve Brazil's debt, what is really being gained? If the same Northern community serves as the headquarters of several multinational companies that employ children in Brazil for 40 cents an hour, is its US–Brazilian sister-city program merely a ruse for continued North–South exploitation?

Questioning Trade

Northern and Southern partners must question trade not only in the abstract but also between their communities. Too often partners assume that any trade relations are beneficial. But whether a trade transaction is really constructive may turn on the following questions: Who gains – the poor or a few elite? What are the environmental and cultural impacts of the production of traded goods? Is the transaction increasing the self-reliance of the partners or creating dangerous dependencies? These questions apply to trade not only between Northern and Southern communities but also between Southern communities.

Many CDI participants in the South would like to see greater South–South trade and advocate South–South twinning as a means to promote it. (South–South trade relations may lead to twinning too; Zambia reported that a number of twinning relationships grew out of its participation in the Southern Africa Development Coordinating Conference and in the Preferential Trade Area.) In theory, South–South trade could enable Southerners to reduce their dependence on the North, to realize more of the gains from trade, and to prevent profiteering by Northern middlemen.

But there are two potential problems with South–South trade, at least as it is currently being conceived. First, it could become a bonanza for Southern elites. Unless the principles of alternative trade also are applied – that is, unless small-scale and cooperative businesses are given priority and profiteering by middlemen is prevented – South–South trade could replicate the worst features of the global economy throughout the South. Preferences for trading should therefore be given to the poor and the dispossessed regardless of where they live. A better model of South–South trade is one in which the poor of the South form ties with the poor of the North to counter the growing power of elites in both regions.

Second, the South should ask whether trade itself is the most desirable direction for development. Might it be more valuable for a community to develop a local economy that does not depend on goods and services from either the North or the South? Seydou Sall of Kenya argues that the grassroots of the South, especially those in Africa, should resist being absorbed into the global marketplace and instead establish their own economic and political institutions. "The role of animators and facilitators who work with grassroots organizations in Africa," writes Sall, "must be to encourage the people to believe in themselves and to build self-confidence in their ability to solve their own problems." South–South cooperation therefore should aim to facilitate, not trade per se, but the exchange of the technology, capital, and people necessary to achieve self-reliance.

Supporting South–South Relations

Even if trade between two communities in the South is of dubious value, other kinds of relations between these communities are unquestionably beneficial. South–South twinning, for example, can help Southern partners experience what it is like to provide valuable assistance to others. Too often, Southern partners are on the receiving end of a relationship, which can lead to feelings of inferiority and resentment. By being able to enter a relationship in which both sides give and take equally, Southern partners can regain their self-confidence. Twinning among Southern partners brings greater understanding, appreciation, and solidarity.

The real value of South–South relations is not that it allows the South to withdraw from the North (which is probably impossible) but that it can help the South restructure its relationship with the North in more just terms. With greater self-sufficiency, the South will be in a stronger position to negotiate its terms of engagement with the North. South–South relations can empower impoverished communities to pool resources, talent, and energy in order to stand up to opposing interests in both the North and the South.

Northern communities might try to help their Southern partners link up with other communities in the South. One worthy goal is to make sure that national governments stay out of the way. Northern communities need to be vigilant, for example, that GATT does not impair the freedom of Southern communities to give contract or investment preferences to Southern companies.

The Bulawayo Appeal also urged Northerners who were "the initiators of this conference to encourage and support similar regional linking-for-development conferences in other parts of Africa, Asia, and Latin America." Certainly this advice remains sound today. Northern communities can show solidarity with the South by raising funds for South–South meetings, partnerships, projects, and trade.

Protecting Human Rights

In the Bulawayo Appeal participants of the South–North International Conference on Linking for Development committed themselves "to the campaign against apartheid, its institutions, and all other forms of racism and oppression, and to the support of all efforts to establish a world in which human rights and dignity are respected and promoted." The Sevagram Declaration from India urged local governments to "have specific projects...on human rights."

In the spirit of these declarations, communities interested in North–South development cooperation have dealt with human-rights issues in three different contexts. First, in recognition that basic civil liberties are required for people-centered development to succeed, some localities have sought to "mobilize shame" against governments to free political prisoners, to end repression, and to dismantle apartheid. Human-rights concerns also have arisen concerning the treatment of refugees within communities. A third context is conflict resolution. To protect the basic rights of citizens not to have their lives shattered by bullets, grenades, or bombs, communities have promoted the peaceful settlement of disputes in Nicaragua, Southern Africa, Northern Ireland, the Middle East, Yugoslavia, and nearly every other war-torn region in the world.

In each of these categories there have been significant successes and failures. Some political prisoners whose cause was adopted by communities have been freed, while others still languish in jail. Thanks to campaigns led by activists within South Africa, and joined by NGOs and communities throughout the world, apartheid has been weakened, though not yet crushed. Local efforts to help refugees certainly have improved the lives of some, but racism and hatred against foreigners remain on the rise. Most community efforts to end conflicts have been on the margins of diplomacy, but it is hard not to be impressed by the fact that more than a hundred East–West sister-city links, supported by thousands of "citizen diplomats," helped end the Cold War. Equally astonishing is that the US–Nicaragua sister-city movement, along with other solidarity groups, convinced the US

Congress to cut off military aid to the contras and effectively end a civil war that claimed 30,000 lives.

Many CDI practitioners are reluctant to add human rights to their agenda, because they fear that controversy will marginalize their CDIs. To fight for human rights abroad is to say, if only implicitly, that one's own government is not doing enough. To lobby for the release of political prisoners means vilifying and confronting another government. To protect refugees means resisting and challenging politically powerful xenophobes. To be a peace-maker means branding governments as aggressors and opposing powerful interests such as arms manufacturers. The highly political tone of these initiatives can be dissonant for the supporters of "mainstream" CDIs such as development education and linking.

But there are two important lessons of the 1980s that can bridge the gap between the skeptics and the supporters of human-rights CDIs. Skeptics should concede that these initiatives have worked often enough to be taken seriously. Supporters should concede that human-rights initiatives can be undertaken in non-partisan, non-confrontational ways that are compatible with other CDIs. This second point warrants elaboration.

Ordinary citizens can help prevent human-rights abuses simply by establishing close ties with potential victims. There was nothing inherently antagonistic about the Norwegian city of Krakeroy's decision to link with the small mountain village of Patzun in Guatemala. But by bearing witness to events in Patzun, by sending visitors regularly, by standing alongside Patzun's leaders, the Norwegian public helped deter Guatemalan army units and death squads from continuing what had been a pattern of harassment and violence.

CDIs that help refugees also need not be confrontational. Festivals involving different ethnic groups can expose the community to the best of these groups' food, music, art, dance, and literature and tear down hateful stereotypes. Moreover, each friendship a community member makes with a refugee has a multiplier effect, reducing local prejudices, fears, and racism.

Even issues of war and peace can be approached in non-confrontational ways. The American and European peace movements began the 1980s by protesting against weapons systems but gradually focused on improving East–West relations. Once peace activism was defined, not just as the absence of weapons and war, but as an ongoing effort to remove the roots of conflict, it became more popular. City councils throughout the United States and Europe that never would have deemed themselves "peaceniks" had no compunction about supporting Soviet sister-city programs. The recent Dutch initiative to use local officials to mediate the Yugoslavian civil war has demonstrated that it is possible to promote conflict resolution without taking sides.

If human-rights initiatives still seem too controversial, a community might choose to launch CDIs that satisfy different constituencies. The city council of Salzburg, for example, mollified conservative opponents of twinning with Nicaragua by setting up another twinning program with Singida in Tanzania that was more to their liking. Both progressives and conservatives in Salzburg thus had CDIs embodying their viewpoints.

There also are a number of very simple initiatives that communities can undertake to enhance public understanding of human rights. Participants at a recent colloquy on "Democracy and Human Rights," held by the Council of Europe's North–South Center in Lisbon, concluded that national governments should translate and distribute these international instruments concerning human rights, promote human-rights education at all levels, organize periodic radio broadcasts on human rights, support human-rights NGOs and citizens' associations, and provide human-rights training for magistrates, lawyers, police officials, prison staff, teachers, and journalists. All these tasks can, and should, be done at the local level. Even ratification, which is normally the prerogative of national governments, can be done symbolically at the local level through city-council resolutions.

Moving Beyond Aid

"While aid is welcome and necessary for those who suffer from injustice," advised the Cologne Appeal, "aid is insufficient for achieving a genuine solution. All too often aid can be used as an alibi to ease the conscience of the North." Despite this strong urging that communities move beyond aid, it is striking and disappointing how many CDIs are primarily aid programs. The report on CDIs in Norway, for example, begins with a brilliant critique of the liabilities of aid but then describes in uncritical terms a dozen linking programs that are little more than creative fund-raising endeavors. Analysts from both the North and South criticize aid programs for continuing patterns of dependence and exploitation, yet most Northern communities continue to give aid and most Southern communities continue to take it.

Nevertheless, it is important to remember that there *is* an inherent inequality between most Northern and Southern communities, and aid is one means of addressing it. As Gladys Maseko, Administrative Secretary for African Community-Based Development Initiatives, writes:

> Twinning/linking has limitations in that it is trying to bring equality to people who are too far apart in their levels of development – socially, economically, technologically, educationally, and in their cultural values. It is inevitable that instead of trying to be equal, as twinning implies, the South will expend itself trying to catch up with the North.

Aid can be especially useful to relieve suffering during a crisis. A recent survey revealed that aid sent to 31 Nicaraguan communities in the 1980s by linking partners in the United States and Western Europe comprised half of their municipal investment. In the poorest of these Nicaraguan communities, aid comprised 90 percent of municipal investment.

Collecting aid also has the virtue of providing Northerners with specific fund-raising tasks. Hanni Nuotio, the Finnish organizer of Espoo's relationship with Ovamboland in Namibia, notes:

> After we decided to switch over from collection of material goods to other types of activities, it was more difficult to engage people. It was so easy and practical to collect goods. Now, things are maybe less concrete, and for many, money seems to be the only way of participating.

The risk of basing North–South cooperation on collecting aid, as the Norwegian city of Kristiansand discovered with its link with Rajshahi in Bangladesh, is that the link can collapse when people get tired of fund-raising. Similarly, the Norwegian city of Nesodden found itself expending so much energy on collecting money for poor women in Bangladesh that the other aspects of the relationship practically disappeared.

Whatever the virtues of aid, communities must recognize that the outflow of resources from South to North is so large that only a massive infusion of aid – far beyond the reach of communities – can possibly reverse it. The 2,000 Northern communities involved in development cooperation *each* would have to contribute $25 million annually just to stop the current hemorrhage of money from South to North.

For people-centered development, what ultimately matters is whether a community is increasing its capacity to manage its own affairs. Aid sometimes can help with this, but more often it is simply consumed. The impulse to send aid, therefore, might be better directed at providing partners with books and teaching materials or with appropriate technology. Two other alternatives to aid also are worth considering: strengthening civil society and initiating alternative trade.

Civil society refers to the capacity of people to solve social problems without national government. In a healthy civil society a wide range of NGOs flourish, including youth groups, AIDS hospices, parent–teacher associations, environmental groups, public charities, and unions. NGOs can solve social problems quickly, amplify the voices of disadvantaged members of the community, and put pressure on government leaders. Consequently, a number of European communities have made development of civil society a central part of their twinning and linking programs. The proliferation of linking projects involving churches, universities, and women's groups is one indication of growing interest in promoting civil society.

Equally important players in civil society are labor unions, political parties, and human-rights groups. The concerted effort by the Association of Netherlands Municipalities to teach civil servants in the East about the virtues of multiparty democracy, due process, free speech, labor rights, and a vigorous volunteer sector is a good example of how to promote civil society through CDIs. Another is the union-to-union linking between Zimbabwe and the Finland National Trade Union of Commerce and Trade.

Alternative trade also should be considered. By buying crafts or commodities such as coffee directly from small-scale or cooperative producers in the South at a higher price, alternative-trade distributors ensure that producers receive a decent wage and that there is no profiteering by middlemen. European communities have supported alternative trade by drinking "solidarity coffee" and selling crafts in "Third World shops." In the coming years the range of products available from alternative trade will probably expand to include cocoa, nuts, and other basic commodities.

Balancing North–South Relations

Although the Cologne Appeal urged that relationships between partners be based on "equality, reciprocity, absence of paternalism," the evidence suggests that this is not occurring. Nearly all North–South twinnings, linkings, or projects that have been reported were initiated by the North. Northerners did most of the traveling and paid for most of the plane fares of Southerners. Northern communities sponsored most of the meetings and conferences concerning CDIs, usually on the North's turf and on the North's terms.

In his paper on "South–North Linking: A Southern Perspective," Peter Nyoni writes:

I observed an emerging contradiction in this enthusiastic North–South movement whose ideal was an equality of relationship between North and South. There had been no…organizational evolution in any one country, continent, or region in the South where there were North–South links that paralleled the process in the North. There certainly were no comparable resources available to the Southern groups as had been available to their counterparts in the North. How, then, could there be a sense of mutual collaboration between communities in the North and in the South in the face of such disparities between them?

To be sure, there have been some noteworthy CDI initiatives from the South. In 1990, when famine hit the town of Dushanbe in the Soviet Union, its Zambian twinning partner, Lusaka, sent shipments of food. CDI practitioners from southern Africa played a leading role in organizing the "Conference on South–North Linking for Development" in Bulawayo, Zimbabwe, and organizers from India put together the Sevagram conference in 1992. Both forums articulated Southern perspectives on how linking could proceed in a more balanced way.

But for complete balance to be restored to these relationships, Northern communities must recognize that there is much they can learn from their Southern partners. The Kirklees Metropolitan Borough in the United Kingdom decided to redesign its youth employment training program after seeing how well its partners in Bulawayo addressed the problem. Italian localities learned from their partners in Rio de Janeiro how to cope with legions of street children. New Haven, Connecticut, got useful tips on how to reorganize its health-care delivery system and its adult-literacy programs from partners in Leon, Nicaragua.

Imbalance taints North–South CDIs. As Gabriel Banda from Zambia notes:

> [T]here may be a need to work towards a level relationship where we interact as friends rather than as juniors and superiors. [We must accept] other towns in places like Zambia as having valid, important experiences we can learn and benefit from. This will also make us value ourselves and our contribution to all towns and development relationships we embark on.

Both a cause and an effect of the current state of imbalance is that CDIs tend to focus on the South's development problems, not the North's. This dynamic of the North "saving" or "helping" the South continues a tradition of exploitation that Northerners practiced as missionaries and conquerors. Northern practitioners of CDIs must stop hiding their own economic, social, and political problems. It is currently estimated, for example, that 100 million people living in the North are destitute.

Perhaps it would be helpful if a greater diversity of Northerners participated in linking programs. Most Northern organizers of CDIs tend to be well educated, middle class (or upper class), and idealistic. They do not well represent their own communities, especially the poor, the homeless, the elderly, the disabled, the unemployed, the sick, and the forgotten.

The diversity of Southern participants also needs to be expanded. Too often, as Mathew Kibe of Kenya reports, municipal officials or other elites from the South try "to monopolise and hijack" linking relationships:

> There have been problems with councillors not understanding why members of the community should be involved in what they perceive to be a municipal affair. When it comes to exchange visits, it is difficult to get them to understand the point as they also like to be involved in exchange visits.

Another way communities can escape the quandary of imbalance is by finding common problems which allow each partner to act on its own. A Northern and a Southern partner can each agree to start its own development education program and to share learning materials. Each can promise to improve its own environmental behavior (the Climate Alliance is a good model). Each can commit itself to lobby national officials for lower levels of military spending or to put parallel sanctions on irresponsible corporations. And each can agree to improve protection for foreign-born minorities living in its jurisdiction.

But some imbalance may be inevitable. The premise of CDIs is that the North has economic and technological endowments that far surpass those of the South. Partners should feel no shame if they decide jointly to build a water system in the South. The key to a good linking relationship, like any good relationship, is that partners remain alert to imbalances and try to minimize them.

Diversifying CDIs

CDI participants are nearly unanimous in proclaiming that the end of the Cold War is having a dramatic effect on CDIs, but they cannot agree on whether this change is good or bad. Some lament that Northern aid which once flowed south is now heading east and that some Northern communities are losing interest in Southern partnerships. If this is true, the South's loss is the East's gain. But if the end of the Cold War leads to deep cuts in military spending, the savings could translate into more resources for both the East and the South.

It is unclear how changing national priorities will affect CDIs. If national governments grow less interested in helping the South, progressive communities in the West may choose to get more involved. After all, visionary communities in the West launched most CDIs because of the failures of national development programs. In London, for example, despite the growing national hostility to refugees and despite diminished power and money for local actions, several boroughs are increasing their commitment to protect and resettle refugees.

There are strong reasons for communities to support linking with the East and the South, and not to pursue one at the expense of the other. The Dutch community of Deventer, which has projects in both Cameroon and Estonia, realized that each relationship involves different members of the community. "Generally speaking," according to John Kuiper of Deventer, "the groups dealing with Southern hemisphere issues consist of younger people to the left of the political scale. Groups whose interest concerns the East seem to appeal to the elderly and are neither on the political left nor right." Another reason to retain partnerships with both East and South is that each program can learn from the other. Cooperation, therefore, not competition, should be the goal. This explains why Deventer decided to allocate separate funds for its Cameroon and Estonian programs.

Another way to avoid competition is to set up a triangular relationship involving communities from the North, South, and East. The Dutch, for example, are putting together projects involving communities from the Netherlands, Nicaragua, and the Czech Republic. The Americans are integrating Eastern and Southern partners with their sister-city ties with Japan. While these triangular relationships pose special logistical, cultural, and political problems, they also add a new exciting dimension to North–South and East–West partnerships. Once participants from the North, South, and East can see that each community comes with special skills and experiences, they understand why it is foolish to drop one partner for another.

Empowering Local Governments

Part of what makes joint action in development cooperation so powerful is the role of local government. Local government can equip CDIs with money, legitimacy, and expertise. But in many countries in both the North and South – such as Greece, India, Japan, and the Philippines – local governments are at a very early stage of political development, with limited power and autonomy. In the absence of national approval, municipal money in these countries cannot be spent on even the simplest development education or twinning programs. "Without adequate power to levy taxes on its citizens," writes Manab Chakraborty of India, "many municipalities of the South remain financially vulnerable. Unless there is a significant devolution of power and decentralisation, popular democratic participation will be difficult in many countries in the South."

A vital task for communities with weak local governments is to convince their national government to decentralize power. They might lobby national officials to adopt and adhere to the Council of Europe's Convention on Local Self-Government (1985) and IULA's Worldwide Declaration of Local Self-Government (1985). But even countries that follow these agreements do not provide their local governments with the full range of powers needed to implement every kind of CDI. Many Western European countries, for example, interpret EC law as forbidding local authorities from boycotting or divesting from corporations on political grounds.

If communities are to exercise meaningful influence over environmental protection, the global economy, and human rights, they should demand the following:

- the power to sponsor public education initiatives, even if the viewpoints presented differ from that of the national government
- the power to lobby national leaders on any issue, including those related to foreign policy
- the power to regulate corporations doing business in the community to protect public health, safety, and welfare
- the power to add political criteria to decisions concerning which companies should receive municipal investment, contracts, or purchases
- the power to raise the revenues necessary for CDIs through progressive taxation.

Those NGOs, cities, and associations of cities that are coordinating CDIs on a nationwide basis can play an important role in promoting these reforms. The Local Government International Bureau (LGIB) in the United Kingdom, for example, worked closely with key parliamentarians to get the House of Commons to consider a bill giving UK local authorities the powers necessary to proceed with overseas assistance.

In short, communities everywhere should demand greater political power. They should do so in their own countries and do so internationally. "Northern institutions, in collaboration with popular grassroots movements," advises Chakraborty, "must press hard simultaneously for democratisation and for empowerment of local structures in the South." Southerners, of course, might similarly assist Northern communities. Communities everywhere should stress that a strong local government allows people to shape their own destiny, while a weak local government surrenders that destiny to distant national, regional, and international bureaucracies.

Building Local Institutions

Special problems begin to beset communities as their CDIs become more numerous and multifaceted. Inefficiencies develop; three linking programs based in one community might attempt to publish three different newsletters rather than work together on a single newsletter. CDIs can work at cross-purposes; the city of Tallahassee, Florida, was recently embarrassed to discover that one branch of its government was divesting funds from firms doing business in South African while another branch was wooing a company with South African ties. And without an open, public institution, a city's international affairs activities can be captured by special interests. Whenever a single group dominates CDIs – whether activists, churches, or businesses – democracy suffers.

To prevent inefficiencies, contradictions, and inadequate representation, some communities have created institutions to devise coherent global policies and to ensure that all community groups are heard. These institutions also provide continuity when political circumstances change. Thus, communities in the North that were formally twinned with Nicaraguan communities survived the change of government in 1990 more easily than those that were informally linked.

A good example of an integrated municipal policy comes from the Dutch city of Groningen, which in 1989 published "The Municipality and Global Awareness-Raising," a comprehensive plan for how the community could promote sustainable development, peace, human rights, and global ecological protection. As a result of that plan, the city now spends more than 300,000 guilders ($162,000) per year on grants for a Third World center, a Third World shop, a peace information center, the Groningen-San Carlos Twinning Project, the Samafco Project (for refugees from Tanzania), and a twinning with Transvaal in South Africa. Each administrative department within the city also designates a civil servant to help formulate the city's global policy, and these departmental liaisons are overseen by a half-time coordinator.

The key elements underlying Groningen's success seem to be an annual plan, the ongoing participation of NGOs and municipal staff, a paid coordinator, and a major budgetary commitment. An additional element that could strengthen Groningen's work would be annual hearings to ensure that all NGOs and community groups within the city have an opportunity to shape and critique the plan. Communities everywhere should consider preparing and disseminating an annual "State of the City in the World" report. Keeping CDIs grounded in local interests is a good way of maintaining popular support. A recurring lesson is that whenever a mayor or city council member tries to craft CDIs without public input or accountability, he or she invites a backlash at the polls.

The need for a budgetary commitment deserves special emphasis, because in many countries the absence of money is one of the biggest obstacles to CDIs. In the United States, for example, the average sister city spends just $10,000 per year, and three out of four raise all of this money from private sources. In Italy limits on public spending imposed by national governments have prevented communities from hiring qualified staff, and to the extent that communities depend on funds from the Italian foreign ministry they remain vulnerable to unexpected delays and bureaucratic snafus. As Mathew Kibe of Kenya writes, "Financial contribution is power." Money is a necessary (though insufficient) condition for "serious" development initiatives, and it is one of the main reasons citizens, NGOs, and community groups turn to local authorities for help.

To increase the financial commitment of Belgian communities to CDIs, NCOS organized a campaign to convince local governments to spend 0.7 percent of their municipal budget on development cooperation (0.7 percent is the percentage of GNP that the United Nations has said countries in the North should spend to promote development in the South). A more modest expenditure goal – "more realistic" is how some communities would put it – is to expend one unit of their national currency per capita. Thus, the 100 largest communities in the Netherlands are now spending each year a guilder per person on CDIs. Similarly, a number of communities in Germany are spending more than DM 1 per capita.

Recruiting National Government Support (Cautiously)

CDIs can clearly benefit if a community has a close, cooperative relationship with its national government. In the Netherlands close ties between local and national authorities have resulted in a generous flow of resources to both NGOs and local authorities in support of CDIs. Cooperation also means that local and national politicians can learn from one another, that educational materials can be developed jointly, that national campaigns can be designed to reach more people, and that national policies can be formulated with greater popular input.

But all national governments dislike some CDIs. The US Justice Department convinced federal courts to invalidate nuclear-free zones and gubernatorial restrictions on militia training in Honduras. Prime Minister Thatcher undercut nuclear-free zones and twinning with Nicaragua when she abolished the Greater London Council and several other municipal governments in the mid-1980s. The Japanese central government has used its financial leverage over local governments to ensure that CDIs promote Japanese business more than people-centered development. Even the Dutch government, which otherwise has been very supportive of CDIs, saw fit to invalidate municipal sanctions against South Africa.

These examples suggest that a community would be wise to inoculate its CDIs from national attack. Protecting certain spheres of municipal power as local rights, as noted earlier, is one good step. Underwriting CDIs with locally raised funds is another.

Still another option is defiance. Some communities have found that waging legal battles with national authorities can educate the public about foreign policy, mobilize sympathetic communities, weaken national leaders, and strengthen the leaders of opposition parties. This was one reason why a number of Dutch communities fighting apartheid continued to explore ways of boycotting Royal Dutch Shell, despite clear government decrees that their actions were illegal. And "radical" movements sometimes win. In the United States divestment against South Africa was begun by a few brave cities, but then snowballed into a gigantic movement that ultimately was ratified by the US Congress.

Confrontation carries risks. Moderates interested in linking complain bitterly that radical initiatives make it more difficult to win support from national or local officials for their CDIs. Whether a community is wiser to influence the national government through collaboration or confrontation depends on particular circumstances within each country. Hundreds of US communities could certainly justify launching antagonistic "municipal foreign policies" in the 1980s, when the nation's foreign policy – a massive arms buildup, "constructive engagement" with South Africa, a covert war against Nicaragua, hostility toward much of the South – was exactly the opposite of the people-centered development agenda. But now that the Cold War is over, apartheid almost dead, Nicaragua at peace, and relations with the South more friendly, US communities believe that compromise and dialogue with national authorities is possible.

European communities generally have been more fortunate than their US brethren to have sympathetic national governments. Even in countries like the United Kingdom where community views deviated substantially from national foreign policies, dissenting communities were able to influence national leaders through strong political parties, through the institutions of the EC, and through national "quadrilogue" structures.

Constructing National, Regional, and International Structures

Where there is no national institution coordinating CDIs, as in Italy, initiatives are fragmentary and spread slowly. Conversely, the quantity and quality of CDIs increase dramatically in countries where there is at least one strong institution documenting, analyzing, and promoting their progress. Sometimes this institution has been a determined NGO, such as NCOS in Belgium, Terre des Hommes in Germany, the Institute for the Study and Documentation of Africa and Latin America (IEPALA) in Spain, Oxfam in the United Kingdom, and the Institute for Policy Studies in the United States. In other instances the key institution has been an NGO receiving major grants from the government, such as NCO in the Netherlands or Sister Cities International in the United States. Local governments may take on this networking role, as Mainz and Bremen have done in Germany. Or associations of cities may play a major role, as have the VNG in the Netherlands and the Local Government International Bureau in the United Kingdom.

Building a network of CDIs through deliberate institutional action is better than leaving their evolution to chance. Regular surveys can increase public interest in CDIs and help win the support of skeptical local politicians. Conferences and seminars enable experienced communities to share what they have learned with inexperienced communities and to goad the latter into action. Quadrilogue structures can recruit more NGOs, communities, parliamentarians, and national bureaucrats. Distribution of the Cologne Appeal, the Berlin Charter, and similar documents can help communities feel part of a global movement. Meetings targeted at specific groups such as local officials, civil servants, or university professors can mobilize their support for CDIs. Leaflets, newsletters, and reports summarizing the accomplishments of CDIs can spread success stories to other communities. And all these activities can be spurred through national co-financing. NCO has convinced two-thirds of the communities in the Netherlands to involve themselves in development cooperation by co-financing 300 to 400 education projects per year and by supporting national surveys, conferences, and booklets.

Of course, the arguments for national coordination apply at the regional level as well. Towns and Development itself is an example of a regional institution creating a regional movement, in part because of co-financing from the Council of Europe and from the European Commission. Other regional institutions supporting CDIs include the North–South Centre of the Council of Europe and Citynet of Asia. The Bulawayo conference, which was partially underwritten by Towns and Development, the Commonwealth Secretariat, Christian Aid, Oxfam-Zimbabwe, and Oxfam-UK, convinced participants to set up an African secretariat that could publish surveys, hold regular conferences, and disseminate reports on CDIs. The Sevagram Declaration suggested "that an office of Towns and Development be established in India."

Finally, truly international organizations of cities may be necessary to spread CDIs throughout the world. The International Union of Local Authorities and the United Towns Organisation have already played a key role. Over time it will be crucial to set up an international secretariat (an organization of communities run for the benefit of communities) to ensure that global problems are met through globally coordinated local action.

●   ●   ●

Will CDI practitioners rise to these 14 challenges? Will they begin to collect data and evaluate their programs more seriously? Will they ensure that development education leads to tough-minded political action? Will they address the issues of unsustainable lifestyles, unfair trade, Third World debt, and human-rights abuses? Will they press twinning and linking relationships to move beyond aid and to become more balanced? Will they construct institutions at the local, national, and international level needed for CDIs to realize their full potential?

The answers to these questions will determine the fate of the CDI movement. Fortunately, the answers do not depend on any arcane theories of political science or economics. They depend on direct action. They depend on you. The challenge for each of us is to organize our own community, to create a working coalition of NGOs and community groups committed to people-centered development, to press our local officials to sponsor as many CDIs as possible, and to give these CDIs real teeth. To help you take the next steps, the Appendices detail what is going on in 22 countries, what resources are available, and who you can contact.

Twenty years ago many despaired that global problems were spinning out of control. But slowly, inexorably, communities have shown that global change is within their power. They have cut the world's problems down to manageable size and exerted influence far in excess of their numbers. They have ended wars, freed political prisoners, cleaned up the global environment, rebuilt villages, and restored hope.

Perhaps most importantly, communities have demonstrated a fundamental new paradigm in international relations. It used to be that we could influence matters outside our country only by appealing to national leaders. We pled with national leaders to stop doing some things, and start doing others. The new paradigm is to take foreign relations into our own hands. Partnerships should be forged with national governments whenever possible, but when they cannot be, communities should move forward anyway – and make sure national officials stay out of the way.

As the late economist Kenneth Boulding once wrote, "Cities of the world unite! You have nothing to lose but your slums, your poverty, and your military expendability."

Country Reports

The following summaries suggest that CDIs are a worldwide phenomenon. In almost every one of the 22 nations examined, local authorities, NGOs, and community groups are engaged in some form of joint action on development issues.

Argentina

Argentinian CDIs first appeared in 1983, when the military dictatorship of Leopoldo Galtieri collapsed and the country began to rebuild its institutions of local governance and civil society. The return of democracy was slow, however, because it coincided with a steadily worsening economic and social crisis, triggered in part by "structural adjustment" measures imposed by the International Monetary Fund and the World Bank.

NGOs were practically non-existent before 1976, when the military came to power. During the dictatorship only a few audacious NGOs dared to go public, usually to protest human-rights violations. It was really after 1983 that NGOs and community groups multiplied dramatically to meet the country's escalating social and economic needs. Environmental groups became popular vehicles for helping the poor and espoused the philosophy of Mrs Maria Onestini, who wrote in her popular book *Environment and Poverty* that "poverty and environmental damage are parallel and intimately related to an inequitable and erroneous development pattern."

Local governments traditionally had little power in Argentina, but the failures of centralized military rule led to a gradual process of democratization and devolution of authority after 1983. Even today, however, many municipalities are quite bureaucratic and paternalistic, and unwilling to work with NGOs and community groups. Moreover, development education – one of the most common CDIs in other countries – barely exists because Argentinian localities do not control the local schools.

Still, there is some evidence of cooperation between municipal authorities and NGOs. In Baradero City, for example, municipal employees used technical advice, materials, and land from the city government to build an independent cooperative with 20 houses. Two Argentinian NGOs (Lihuen Antu and Fundacion del Sur) and two European NGOs (Fundacion CIPIE from Spain and SAILD from Italy) worked with the Epuyen Municipio to create a cattle and agricultural development program. After squatters illegally occupied an old municipal building in Buenos Aires, city officials decided to help them refurbish the structure.

Perhaps the most significant joint action with Northern groups has taken place to protect the environment. The biggest environmental polluters in Argentina have been corporations from the North, and important allies for clean-up campaigns have been Northern NGOs and governments. Three examples illustrate the complex interplay of Northerners and Argentina's environmental problems.

When the news reached Moreno Municipio that a German company was about to build a factory to treat toxic wastes from Northern countries, all hell broke loose. A community group called "Committee for Environmental Protection" mobilized neighborhoods to protest the project, and with the help of Greenpeace Latin America and Fundacion del Sur they convinced city officials to declare Moreno an "ecological protected zone." Other communities passed similar laws and successfully pressed the National Congress to prohibit the importation of toxic wastes into any part of Argentina.

The municipality of Sierra del Medio in the Patagonian Region opposed the plans of the National Committee of Atomic Energy (CNEA) to establish a nuclear-waste repository. A community group called Movimiento Antinuclear Chabut organized rallies and parades and gathered 15,000 signatures to halt the project. Other NGOs joined in, including the World Council of Indian Groups, which was concerned that the repository would displace native peoples. Two hundred kilometers away Chilean NGOs also demanded that the project be scrapped, and more than a dozen other Argentinian municipalities declared themselves "non-nuclear" communities in solidarity with the protestors. Despite heavy lobbying by Northern companies to proceed with the radioactive dump, the national government suspended the project indefinitely.

An NGO called CEDEA recently began a clean-up of the Matanza-Riachuelo River, which runs through Buenos Aires. Companies throughout the region, including 40 foreign-owned enterprises, had been dumping untreated sewage, solid wastes, petroleum, slaughterhouse remains, and other contaminants into the waterway. National legislation in 1978 required polluting industries to clean up their wastes or pay compensation, but to the dismay of the residents of Buenos Aires most of the firms along the Matanza-Riachuelo River decided to pay and go on polluting. CEDEA documented the case and presented it to the Second International Water Tribunal, with the help of the government of the Netherlands and Dutch NGOs.

Argentinian NGOs and local authorities found that, working together, they could influence public awareness and national policy. Even though the municipalities lacked the legal authority to shut down hazardous industries, their campaigns with NGOs enabled them to generate enough local, regional, and national criticism to do essentially the same thing. Northern NGOs played a critical role in helping these initiatives to succeed.

Austria

Three types of CDIs predominate in Austria: development education, environmental initiatives, and twinning.

Austrian schools integrated North–South issues into their curricula in the 1980s. This was not always easy because of the rigidity of the country's education system; interdisciplinary teaching and project-oriented classes, for example, are discouraged. As students and teachers became more interested in global development, they began to link up with schools and adopt projects in the South, all of which attracted press attention.

In 1989 the Austrian Information Service on Development Politics began recruiting communities for the Climate Alliance, and 20 have joined since. Members of the alliance educate the Austrian public on deforestation and provide financial support for rainforest-preservation projects in the South. The Tropical Timber Campaign also is widely supported in the country.

Twenty Austrian cities are twinned with communities in the South – seven with Africa and 13 with Nicaragua. Half are officially recognized. The first twinning began in 1978, when a student in Murzzuschlag won a radio-announcing contest and called for a greater Austrian commitment to development aid. Citizens in Murzzuschlag responded positively, and with the help of a NGO called Third World Platform they identified Arusha in Tanzania as a good twinning partner. Local newspapers and radio stations raised funds for the program, and city council members set a positive example for citizen contributions by donating part of their living allowances.

Austrians initiated all but one of the country's 20 twinning relationships. Generally the key movers were politicians, solidarity groups, or the youth organizations of political parties. The Social Democratic Party, for example, organized a number of Austria's more controversial links with Nicaragua. The accomplishments of these twinnings have been impressive. Through private donations and grants from local authorities and the national government, Leibnitz has given a million dollars in assistance to Pedra Badejo in Cape Verde. The Salzburg–Leon twinning is an umbrella for 15 links between Austrian and Nicaraguan schools, universities, youth groups, and parishes. NGOs and community groups throughout the country are raising public consciousness through newsletters, newspaper articles, cultural festivals, slide-shows, and solidarity weeks.

Three Austrian organizations promoted CDIs in 1988 and 1989: the Austrian Federation of Towns, the Center for Urban Studies and Documentation, and the Austrian Information Service for Development Policy (an umbrella group with more than a thousand NGO members). These networking institutions ran CDI conferences, designed poster campaigns, and set up a working group with representatives from NGOs, local governments, and official development agencies. More recently, the Vienna Institute for Development and Cooperation has become the principal national promoter of CDIs. The Austrian National Quadrilogue, established in 1991, also has facilitated joint action.

While CDI practitioners in Austria are satisfied that they have raised public consciousness about North–South issues and helped their partners in the South, there are worrisome trends as well. It is getting harder to recruit volunteers. Public interest is drifting from South to East. And the escalating costs of resettling immigrants from the East and cleaning up local ecological messes are leaving less money in municipal budgets for CDIs.

Belgium (Flanders)

CDIs have a long history in the Flanders region of Belgium, where villages have been sending missionaries to the South for hundreds of years. Starting in 1965, a number of development-oriented NGOs formed the NCOS (the National Center for Development Cooperation) to recruit communities for the 11.11.11 Campaign. As detailed in Chapter 2, the 11.11.11 Campaign asks citizens in Flanders to contribute money or take some action for development in the South every year at 11 a.m. on November 11th. In the weeks and months leading up to this moment, communities sponsor activities that raise public awareness on North–South issues.

In 1973 NCOS demanded that candidates for local office declare their views on development cooperation. During the 1980s it published and disseminated a brochure entitled "The Third World in the Council Chamber" and a booklet on "Development Cooperation" (part of a series called *The Municipal Policy in Practice*). As a result of NCOS's educational and lobbying work, all the political parties in Flanders now regularly take positions on development cooperation, and all of them agree that municipalities should be involved.

As discussed earlier, NCOS has been especially successful in building municipal institutions for CDIs. Nearly all of the 308 communities in Flanders allocate a part of the municipal budget for CDIs and designate an alderman to take responsibility for implementing a comprehensive CDI policy.

With the support of NCOS, development-oriented NGOs have formed local "Third World Committees" to amplify their voices. In 1988 NCOS orchestrated a campaign in which these committees demanded that 0.7 percent of the municipal budget be spent on development cooperation. In larger cities these committees became formal advisory boards to the city council called GROS (Municipal Advisory Board for Development Cooperation). Brugge established the first such board in 1976, and other cities followed in the late 1980s. NCOS has five provincial secretaries to coordinate these boards (one for each of the five provinces in Flanders: Antwerp, Brabant, Limburg, Oost-Vlaanderen, and West-Vlaanderen).

NCOS has published regular reports on CDIs to nudge municipalities to become more active and has held seminars and established working groups for city clerks and aldermen. It now finds itself in the "untenable" position of advising all the political parties in Austria, all the Third World clerks, all the GROS and community boards, and all the 11.11.11 committees. Many communities, in turn, pay a tithe to NCOS. NCOS predicts that its monopoly will not last much longer as other NGOs enter the field and as communities grow more confident with their development initiatives.

Following the custom of sending missionaries abroad, most Flanders municipalities provide funds for local citizens or groups to work in the South (some communities provide material support as well). Most cities also give grants to the 11.11.11 committees, as well as to NGOs such as the Belgian Committee for UNICEF, the Foster Parents Plan International, Vredeseilanden (which raises money for projects it calls "isles of peace"), and Damiaanaktie (which fights leprosy). Some of the larger cities like Brugge have created their own NGOs, with several board seats reserved for aldermen and town councilors.

There are also examples of Flanders localities experimenting with more politically daring CDIs. Some have opened up their City Halls to local chapters of Amnesty International for letter-writing campaigns. Five Belgian city councils voted for their jurisdictions to stop purchasing South African fruit. A number of cities no longer use tropical timber in municipal projects. As part of a campaign to stop deforestation in Haiti, 172 municipalities in Flanders planted trees in both Belgium and Haiti, and 60 of these passed resolutions demanding that the Belgian government push for stronger international measures to protect rainforests.

Several Belgian NGOs such as Pax Christa and VAKA have pressured municipalities to enact local peace policies, though the results have been limited. The Third World Council of Brugge was unable to persuade the city to close off its harbor to international arms traffic. Peace activists had better luck convincing Belgian cities to send emergency aid packages to Eastern Europe (though they were criticized by development-oriented NGOs who did not want North–South program funds diverted to East–West programs).

Canada

As members of an ethnically diverse and multilingual society, Canadians have long been interested in international affairs – an interest shared, according to a 1985 survey, by a large number of Canadian municipalities. Unlike many other Northern countries, Canada does not carry the burden of a colonialist past. Nor has it aspired to wield military, political, or economic leverage over developing countries as has its superpower neighbor to the south. These attributes have imbued Canadians with a strong commitment to people-centered development.

The motives for the involvement of Canadian municipalities in North–South development cooperation are similar to those found elsewhere: a genuine humanitarian concern about people living in poverty; a recognition that cities have important expertise to share in an increasingly urbanized world; a desire to improve Canada's position in world trade; an interest in exposing young Canadians to other cultures, races, and languages; and a hope that establishing links between new Canadian immigrants and their homelands can improve racial and ethnic relations within Canada.

The main coordinating body for CDIs has been the Federation of Canadian Municipalities (FCM), which has 600 members. The International Office of FCM acts as a clearing-house for all Canadian twinnings. It advertises Southern requests for twinning partners in its bimonthly magazine *Forum*, and uses its international contacts to locate partners for Canadian cities. In 1988 FCM reported that Canadian cities had 226 twinning relationships abroad, 40 of which were with communities in the South. With financial support from the Canadian International Development Agency (CIDA), FCM now runs three programs relating to North–South cooperation: Municipal Professional Exchange, Africa 2000, and Chinese Open Cities.

In 1986 FCM joined with the Canadian Association of Municipal Administrators to begin the Municipal Professional Exchange Program. This program helped seven Canadian cities swap senior managerial and technical staff with cities in Brazil, China, Colombia, Ghana, India, Senegal, and Zimbabwe. Canadian municipal professionals traveled to Asia, Africa, and Latin America to share their experience with counterparts in the South, and these counterparts then came to Canada for hands-on training. "Professional exchange," says an FCM handbook on *Aid and Trade*, "is a low cost method of establishing strong ties with Third World countries. Apart from the advantages to [these Southern countries], it positions Canada for future trade opportunities and provides professional development opportunities for senior Canadian personnel."

An example of how the Municipal Professional Exchange Program works is the relationship between Calgary, Alberta, and the city of Daqing in China. Using contacts established through twinning, Daqing officials approached Calgary for technical assistance to expand their water supplies that could be used for drinking and for pumping oil out of the ground. The Calgary Economic Development Authority responded by assembling a consortium of local companies for the job and getting FCM to underwrite the training costs for Chinese municipal officers to participate. Today, the water project in Daqing is proceeding, and members of the consortium have taken on other projects in China as well. The mayor of Calgary estimates that the Calgary–Daqing link has resulted in $100 million-worth of business for his community.

Also started in 1986 was the Africa 2000 Program, which the then Canadian minister for external relations and international development described as a "fifteen year commitment by the government of Canada to the recovery and long-term development of Africa." CIDA allocated $150 million for Africa 2000 over the period 1990–95, $10 million of which was for FCM's "Municipal Response." This program currently exchanges municipal professionals (and sometimes community members), supports local environmental assessments by partner cities in Africa, provides modest grants for capital expenditures such as office equipment (up to $25,000 per link), and finances small community projects (up to $20,000 per link in matching funds). (For more details on this program, see Chapter 2.) Thirty-two Canadian cities are participating in the program now, and 50 are expected to be involved by 1995.

An example of the Africa 2000 Program is the link between Nelson, British Columbia, and Mutare, Zimbabwe. In 1989 Donna MacDonald, a member of the Nelson city council, began twinning ties with Mutare, a town she had visited some years earlier when she was studying in Africa. She chose Mutare because, like Nelson, it was located in a mountain range and its economy was based on forestry, mining, and tourism. With funding from the Africa 2000 Program, Nelson sent city staff to Mutare and provided their partners with computers, a fax machine, and spare parts for vehicles. Community groups in Nelson raised $10,000 to help Mutare build a marketplace for women. The link also facilitated church and school links, youth exchanges, and development-education programs. Both sides consider the linking a success, though Gladys Maseko, the Administrative Secretary for Africa Community-based Development Initiatives, criticizes both partners for being preoccupied with material gain.

A third FCM area of activity is called Chinese Open Cities. This program began in 1987 at the request of the Chinese government, which was seeking managerial and administrative expertise for local governments in two dozen areas that were "open" to trade with the outside world (14 coastal cities, four "special economic zones," and three delta areas.) With a five-year budget of $7 million from CIDA, the program brought Chinese local officials, business leaders, and other professionals to Canadian cities for training seminars, study tours, and municipal attachments. The fields covered by teachers included city management, environmental protection, and international trade and finance.

A number of Canadian municipalities also are involved in development education. The country has an annual International Development Week which provides an opportunity for local authorities to raise public consciousness. In 1991, 70 municipalities issued proclamations in support of the week, and many held public exhibitions on North–South topics.

In response to the strong interest of Canadian municipalities to protect the environment, FCM has set up a special environmental office (separate from the international office) which serves as a national clearing-house for information on municipal programs concerning curbside recycling, energy conservation, backyard composting, toxic-waste disposal, and reforestation. One of the "guidelines" which FCM pushes Canadian cities to meet is to reduce carbon-dioxide emissions by 20 percent by the year 2005. The city of Toronto has an especially strong program to fight global warming and in 1991 promised nearly $1 million to establish a headquarters for the International Council for Local Environmental Initiatives (ICLEI).

Some Canadian communities have focused their CDIs on more politically controversial global issues. The Toronto water board decided not to do business with companies involved in South Africa. Several cities have set up links with war-torn El Salvador. With prodding from peace groups, jurisdictions in which two-thirds of the Canadian public now lives have declared themselves "nuclear-free." Montreal passed an ordinance that bans the transportation of nuclear weapons and prohibits municipal purchasing from firms which manufacture nuclear weapons. The provincial legislature of British Columbia recently demanded a full public environmental review of the dangers from nuclear-powered and nuclear-weapons-capable ships and submarines entering its waters. And a number of communities passed resolutions calling for an end to the US–Canadian testing of cruise missiles.

Chile

Chile is now removing the remnants of 16 years of dictatorship under General Augusto Pinochet, whose repressive rule ended in 1989. As the country rebuilds its institutions of local governance and civil society, the stage is being set for joint action at home and abroad.

Chile is divided into 13 regions (run by *intendentes*), 51 provinces (run by governors), and 335 *communes* (run by *alcaldes*). Traditionally the alcaldes were elected, except in the major cities, where they were appointed by the president. Under Pinochet, however, the military appointed all the alcaldes, suppressing the normal mechanisms of local democratic accountability. At the same time Pinochet's neoliberal economic policies led to the transfer of public education, health care, and welfare responsibilities to the municipalities.

NGOs and community groups were all but decimated during the dictatorship, except for those that monitored and controlled dissent. Despite the hostile environment, however, a few bold community groups undertook to provide food, health care, and job training, often with the support of European NGOs and governments. It was not until the final years of Pinochet's rule that NGOs and community groups began to establish working relations with local authorities.

Under Pinochet, decision-making in local authorities was characterized by capriciousness, corruption, bureaucracy, paternalism, and repression. Only recently have some municipalities begun to encourage genuine participation by the citizenry.

In 1990 Gonzalo Duarte, alcalde of the Commune of La Florida, invited all the social organizations in the town to participate in a public discussion of local problems. This process of setting priorities became institutionalized in the Union Communal de Juntas de Vecinos. One concrete result was a housing program for the poor, and more than 600 other projects suggested by social organizations are now being considered by La Florida officials.

The Commune of Conchali created a special municipal department and training program to help its citizens get involved in community development. Thus far, Conchali civil servants and NGOs have teamed up to work on problems of homelessness, illness, illiteracy, and pollution.

In 1991 Sady Melo, alcalde of the Commune of El Bosque, took several major steps to change public attitudes about the municipality. He enlisted NGOs to work with city officials to improve health care, to provide job training for the young, and to beautify the city's environment. One of the popular slogans in the town is "Hagamos de El Bosque un bosque" ('We will turn El Bosque into a forest').

Local democratization of Chile remains a formidable challenge. Pinochet retains some power, authoritarian structures are still embedded in the political system, young vigilantes are stoking public fears, and the population is becoming increasingly apathetic. The need for a revitalization of community politics, particularly by NGOs and community groups, has never been greater. As Mario Garces has written, "There will not be substantial democratization of Chilean society if the popular sectors do not participate in an active way."

Finland

Even though Finnish communities have more than 500 official "friendship cities' in 30 countries, only 15 links – less than 3 percent – are with developing countries. Five of these are with Tanzania, one with Zambia, one with Mozambique, five with Nicaragua, and two with China. In addition, there are ten unofficial North–South links. Nearly all of these were formed after the mid-1980s.

Until recently, the president's strong power over foreign policy seemed to exclude CDIs. But in 1986 dozens of communities organized activities around the United Nations International Year of Peace, the most common of which was to link up with a community in the South. The Association of Finnish Municipalities supported this movement by sponsoring a seminar on the role of municipalities in "peace work," which it defined broadly to include North–South linking.

In June 1988 the Association sent a "recommendation" to Finnish cities, urging them to adopt CDIs, along with a copy of the Cologne Appeal in Finnish. This recommendation stressed that links with the South should employ joint action with NGOs. The Association and Kepa, an umbrella organization for 140

Finnish NGOs involved in North–South development cooperation, formally joined Towns and Development in 1989.

One of the first Finnish North–South links was the city of Espoo's (population 170,000) informal relationship with Nyango, a refugee camp of Namibians in Zambia. The citizens of Espoo sent material aid collected at schools and municipal offices and then designed a special stove for their partners.

When the refugees returned to their home in Ovamboland after Namibia became independent, Espoo helped the women living there create a "model garden" of vegetables and fruit trees appropriate for their desert environment. FINNIDA (the Department for Development Cooperation within the Ministry of Foreign Affairs) gives Espoo $50–70,000 annually for the project, which pays for, among other things, a full-time project coordinator.

The relationship of Oulu (population 100,000) with Matagalpa in Nicaragua originated in 1986 during the International Year of Peace discussions. Oulu has helped its partners in Matagalpa by donating an ambulance, sending volunteers to repair school buildings, and providing monetary assistance to construct streets, sewers, and water-sanitation systems. The city gives $3,000 per year to finance the Oulu–Matagalpa Friendship Association and $7,000 per year to ship a large container of aid. Collections, concerts, and other campaigns generate an additional $10–15,000-worth of assistance annually. The mayors have visited each other, and cultural exchanges have included photo and art exhibitions.

The link of Tampere (population 150,000) with Mwanza in Tanzania also began during the International Year of Peace. While Tampere decided not to spend municipal funds on the link, it helped raise $25,000 by donating proceeds from the sale of 500 Christmas trees harvested from city lands. This money was then used to plant 200,000 trees in Mwanza. (Similar Christmas tree campaigns have been organized for other Finnish twinning projects.) Finnish students, a radio journalist, and the head of the Tampere municipal forestry department have visited Mwanza, but so far no Mwanzans have come to Finland – a serious shortcoming, according to Risto Isomaki, the principal organizer of the link.

In 1988 Kemi, a harbor city in northern Finland, decided to link up with the coastal city of Nacala, Mozambique. This twinning has been characterized by the extensive involvement of the mayors and civil services of both cities. Kemi has established a special office for "close-range democracy and development cooperation," which is run by a city official. In 1990 the partners signed a detailed agreement to exchange information in the fields of engineering and city planning.

School-to-school and union-to-union linkings comprise two other important Finnish CDIs. The National Trade Union of Commerce and Trade reached out to its counterpart in Zimbabwe, and ten of its local branches are now linked together with union branches in Africa.

The future of CDIs in Finland is unclear. Recent economic problems in the country, caused by the collapse of the Soviet Union, have led to "temporary cuts" in national support for development cooperation. In a survey of 94 cities conducted by the Association of Finnish Municipalities in 1990, 26 said they were ready to exchange engineers and other experts with a Southern partner (especially if there was national funding), nine said they wanted to create a North–South link, but 62 said they were not interested in North–South activity.

France

Most CDIs in France are overseen by the United Towns Organisation (UTO) in which 700 French cities are members. Many of these cities have established ties with the Francophone countries of Africa, such as Algeria, Burkina Faso, Mali, Mauritania, Morocco, Senegal, and Tunisia. For a number of years UTO brought together groups of Northern and Southern local elected officials for technical cooperation and consultation, but it was not until 1987, after a conference at Nouakchott, that NGOs were deliberately included. UTO's philosophy has been that twinning partners should promote mutual respect, engage in two-way learning, strengthen institutions of local democracy, and raise community awareness about international affairs.

Another key promoter of French CDIs has been the Programme Solidarite Eau (PSE), which identifies and builds projects to improve water management in the South. Founded in 1984, PSE receives funds from NGOs, local authorities, the Ministry of Development Cooperation, and the Ministry of Foreign Affairs. By 1990 about 400 French communities were participating. But a PSE survey in 1991 revealed that, while local authorities tended to be more involved in large cities and community groups more involved in small towns, NGOs were not participating at any level, even when funds were available.

PSE called together a meeting of the leading French NGOs – Eau Vive, Groupe Recherche Developpement, Cimade Secours Catholique, Comite France contre la Faim, and Association France Volontaire des Progres – to find out why they were uninterested in CDIs. Representatives of these groups complained that they had neither the money nor the staff time to start new activities. They also had concerns about working with smaller cities that lacked experience, sophistication, and long-term commitment. Nevertheless, the NGOs came out of the meeting agreeing to work more closely with municipalities.

A third French organization promoting CDIs is Programme Solidarite Habitat (PSH). Started by the Ministry of Foreign Affairs, which provides 6 million francs ($1.1 million) each year, the program enables local authorities and NGOs to collaborate in the fields of housing and settlement, mainly in Latin America.

In 1989 the Ministry of Development Cooperation established the Commission of Decentralised Cooperation for Development, which included representatives from various national ministries and from local authorities. Working groups within the Commission prepared a CDI guidebook for local authorities and organized training programs for Northern and Southern local elected officials. The

Commission ceased to operate in 1991, but the representative of the Ministry of Foreign Affairs who served on the Commission continues to act as a liaison between local governments and national policy-makers.

Beginning in 1981 about 400 associations sprang up called "Citizens for the Village of …," connecting the 4 million foreign-born people living in France with their brethren abroad. The Panos Institute, studying 15 of these associations, found that 1,294 Africans working in France had sent 4 million francs ($700,000) to their home towns, often with the help of NGOs and municipalities.

Germany

Prior to reunification of Germany nearly all CDIs originated from the western part of the country, where more than 500 out of a total of 8,507 communities were involved in development cooperation. (Today, Germany has 16,314 municipalities.) Consequently, this summary focuses on the evolution of CDIs in West Germany.

Before the 1980s CDIs were practically unheard of. Development cooperation remained in the hands of NGOs and the Federal Ministry of Economic Cooperation. Municipalities believed they had no authority to practice any kind of foreign policy whatsoever. The few CDIs that communities undertook were within the framework of existing town twinnings. NGOs also worried that joint action with governmental bodies would dilute or coopt their goals. But three events catalyzed cooperation between NGOs and municipalities.

The first was the campaign for Towns and Development, spearheaded in Germany by Gunther Hilliges, head of the Bremen State Office of Development Cooperation. Widespread discussion of the Cologne Appeal legitimated the notion that development cooperation should not be left solely to the national government.

The second event was the Practical Solidarity Campaign, initiated by the Council of European Municipalities and Regions. This campaign initially provided aid to impoverished areas of Southern Europe, but under the leadership of Dr Josef Hofmann it gradually extended its reach to other parts of the world. German municipalities recently have cut back their Practical Solidarity work, focusing instead on aiding former East German communities and on helping local refugees who are seeking political asylum.

The third event was the North–South campaign of the Council of Europe, in which municipalities teamed up with NGOs and community groups in "North–South forums" starting in 1988. For the first time small organizations were able to see beyond their narrow agendas and to work with one another and with local authorities. Another important component of the North–South campaign was the "quadrilogue" structure set up by the Council of Europe to facilitate discussion of North–South issues by parliamentarians, governments,

NGOs, and local authorities. These forums enabled information and ideas to flow more smoothly in two directions: from people to governments, and from governments to the people.

German localities initially avoided legal problems by carefully placing expenditures on CDIs within the framework of town twinning. But in October 1988 the prime ministers of the federal states issued a declaration that

> cooperation with less developed countries must enjoy the support not only of the Federal Government and the States, but also of the general public. The States therefore welcome and promote the commitment of NGOs and churches in development cooperation as well as the activities of municipal bodies and initiatives by concerned citizens.

The prime ministers specifically supported "the increased integration of the subject of development policies in information and educational activities both in schools and in the general public in order to deepen the awareness and understanding of the problems of the countries of the Third World."

Most German CDIs fall into three categories: project support, linking/twinning, and information/education. The most popular type of CDI is to provide money for projects in the South or to conduct training courses for Southern administrators and civil servants. Germans like these projects because they are concrete and the benefits are easy to see.

The long, positive experience Germans had forming jumalages with France left them favorably inclined toward twinning with the South. But only a relatively small number of German communities participated; in 1986, 1,240 German communities had jumalages with France, while only 80 were twinned with cities or villages in the South.

Fewer than 100 German municipalities have active public education programs focusing on North–South issues, and only some of these involve close collaboration with NGOs and community groups. Bremen, Frankfurt, Nurnberg, and Krefeld were part of the Towns against Apartheid Campaign, which combined public education with both boycotts of South African fruit and linkings with the frontline states. Bremen and Munich also joined the European campaign not to use tropical timber for municipal construction projects.

No one organization has taken full responsibility for tracking and promoting German CDIs, though the European Office of Communal Development Cooperation of the City of Mainz, headed by Gerold Weisrock, has served informally as an contact point. Three local government associations – the German Cities Association, the German Association of Towns and Municipalities, and the German Association of Counties – also assist with networking.

Greece

CDIs thus far have made relatively little headway in Greece, though some local authorities are beginning to show interest in development education. The country has been so preoccupied with its own development that the national government has yet to formulate a coherent policy toward developing countries. Moreover, the concepts of "NGOs" and "independent local governments" are still new and unfamiliar to most Greeks.

Nevertheless, the Hellenic Institute of Cooperation and Solidarity with Developing Countries (HELLINAS) has begun to promote CDIs through public education, school linking, seminars, conferences, and a magazine called *Synergasia: Cooperation North–South*. HELLINAS has been simultaneously trying to push popular organizations, local governments, and the national government into the field of development cooperation. One of its arguments is that the recent experiences of Greek local governments with their own development, such as their efforts to improve small-scale agriculture, could be valuable to partners in the South.

But HELLINAS faces an uphill struggle. A recent survey found that local authorities give CDIs low priority and that no Greek community has yet participated in a North–South development project, even indirectly by supporting development-oriented NGOs. On the positive side, HELLINAS has recruited ten local authorities to participate in seminars on North–South issues. One of these seminars produced a mandate for local action on environmental protection that was endorsed by the mayor of Athens.

India

In the country with the second largest population in the world (850 million people), CDIs have been surprisingly rare. Only a dozen major cities have twins in Europe, North America, and Africa, and a small number of villages have projects supported by European NGOs and community groups. What *is* noteworthy, however, is an emerging network of NGOs and local authorities promoting people-centered development within India, sometimes with assistance from Northern NGOs.

Efforts to build linkages between India's NGOs and local authorities can be traced to "social work education" that began in Bombay in 1936. These courses taught students how to promote urban and rural development through "community organization," self-reliance, public awareness, and campaigning. Graduates not only exerted influence over government decision-makers; many also became key decision-makers themselves.

NGOs and local authorities recently cooperated to oppose large-scale development projects such as the Tehri Dam and the Narmada Sarovar Project. They also collaborated to address the problems of street children in Bombay and to provide literacy and housing for the poor in Nagpur.

The obstacles facing grassroots activity in India are considerable. Widespread poverty, myriad religious and cultural practices, and 14 major languages (and 200 minor ones) all make organizing on any scale a formidable task.

Some local officials are trying to improve their ties with NGOs through study groups, conferences, and "dialogues." In at least a few instances coalitions of NGOs and local governments have convinced the national government to stop controversial development projects, such as a road that was being built with sub-standard materials and a power station that was spewing uncontrolled emissions of ash.

Supporters of CDIs in India took a great leap forward in March 1992 when 126 delegates from local authorities, NGOs, and community groups attended a four-day meeting in Sevagram to discuss joint action. They resolved, among other things, to set up a Towns and Development chapter in India.

Italy

Several different factors caused Italians to take an interest in CDIs. Italian cities have recently become vocal advocates for decentralizing governmental functions. They have started community-based education programs on peace and development issues. They have assisted the victims of disasters like the war in Biafra and earthquakes in Central America and Algeria. They have absorbed a growing number of refugees from the South, particularly from Latin America. And they have received a growing number of requests from church groups and NGOs to embark on "solidarity" activities with liberation movements abroad and with countries just winning their independence.

Despite these factors, however, there is not yet an organized movement of Italian local authorities and NGOs working together on development cooperation. In fact, until 1987 local authorities had very little power to conduct international relations at all. The only CDIs possible were exchanges of delegations of local officials, and the legal status of even these was unclear. In 1987 the national government clarified the law and gave provincial and local authorities permission to engage in development education, to set up cultural exchanges, and to assist communities in the South through studies, technical assistance, internships, and project support. Since this decree, CDIs have spread rapidly.

In 1988, for example, three Italian councils (Cavamanara, Dorno, and Gropello Cairoli) became twinned with three villages in Senegal after several solidarity groups had laid the groundwork. The Italian side of the relationship is now overseen by a working committee made up of provincial administrators, council members from all three communities, and representatives of the solidarity groups and a local UNICEF chapter. These twinnings begat public education programs about Senegal, exchanges of young Italians and Senegalese, and technical assistance to help Senegalese farmers grow rice and breed livestock. Italian participants also started a "Return of Talent" program that gives recent Senegalese immigrants the opportunity to go back to Senegal with new skills and a modicum of economic security. Financing for the project comes from the Foreign Ministry, which is providing 600 million lire ($485,000) over three years, and from town councils.

Almost every Italian community involved in CDIs has some kind of development-education program, and many are financed by the Foreign Ministry. Invariably these have led to school-to-school linkings, such as the three-way relationship among Milan, Reggio Calabria in southern Italy, and Villa El Salvador in Peru (see Chapter 2 for details).

A number of Italian municipalities also have provided technical and financial assistance to communities in the South. The city of Marsciano financed the construction of a health center in Loropeni, a town in the southern part of Burkina Faso. Legnano, after initially providing medicines and other material support to the municipality of Ebolowa in Cameroon, is now helping its partners build a city hall with a grant of 620 million lire ($501,000) from the Italian Foreign Ministry.

Not all has gone smoothly for Italian CDIs. There is very little coordination among participating cities, and the 150 NGOs involved in development cooperation rarely work together. Serious evaluation of programs is practically non-existent. National restrictions on public spending by local governments prevent communities from hiring qualified staff to oversee their CDI programs. And the dependence of these programs on financing from the Foreign Ministry leaves them vulnerable to unexpected delays and bureaucratic bottlenecks.

But with the help of the National association of Italian Councils, CDIs are beginning to gather some momentum. The association's monthly newsletter, which reaches most local officials, is raising awareness and interest throughout the country about the role Italian towns can play in promoting people-centered development.

Japan

The Japanese government is currently going to great lengths to "internationalize" the country – an effort as ambitious and revolutionary as the "westernization" that took place during the nineteenth century under the Meiji restoration. Local authorities are playing a role in this campaign, though a limited one. Of the 3,250 local governments in Japan, fewer than 10 percent are involved in CDIs. Community-based activities have tended to fall into four categories.

First, with support from the Ministry of Foreign Affairs, the Official Development Assistance (ODA) program has given 47 prefectures and nine major cities the financing to receive trainees from the South. Some prefectures and cities are also sending staff to Southern cities as technical advisors, consultants, and volunteers.

A second category of CDI activity has been sister cities with China, which began after Chairman Mao opened the Peoples Republic to foreign trade and visitors in the 1970s. Some of the Japanese communities participating in these twinnings now receive Chinese trainees.

Japanese NGOs have sown the seeds for a third kind of CDI. Although Japan has more than two hundred development-oriented NGOs, most are quite small and only a few have adopted a community-based approach. But a handful of community groups and NGOs, with the support of local governments, are bringing in trainees from the South or supporting the settlement of Southern refugees in Japan. Because of the difficulty of the Japanese language, localities are inclined to train foreign students who are already studying in Japan.

Japanese chambers of commerce have initiated a fourth kind of CDI: bringing in workers from abroad to meet the country's labor shortage. To skirt the law, which prohibits unskilled laborers from entering Japan, community agencies – with tacit support from the national and local governments – have brought in guest workers under the title of "trainees."

The motivations for Japanese CDIs have been varied. Most of the technical assistance programs were initiated because the national governments asked local governments to help. Some of the larger cities and prefectures have been trying to improve their image for business and tourist purposes. Smaller towns and villages are using CDIs to reenergize their aging populations. Above all, the crucial reason CDIs occur is "personal': the right person in the right position decides to push for a program.

Thus far, CDIs in Japan have been limited to awareness-raising, linking/twinning, and project support, and even in these areas only a few local authorities have taken serious initiatives. There are few examples of development education, lobbying/campaigning, and sanctions. An exception, however, is municipal work on peace. Twelve prefectures and a third of the municipalities in the country have declared themselves nuclear-free, and the cities of Hiroshima and Nagasaki have extensive public education programs advocating nuclear disarmament.

Perhaps the region with the most active development education program is Kanagawa Prefecture. Over the past decade it has held a development-education conference, joined with various NGOs to publish booklets on North–South cooperation, and studied the Korean and Chinese minorities who have settled in the region. The Kanagawa Board of Education also has promoted global peace, human rights, and development cooperation. Another active city has been Sapporo, which has sponsored lectures, movies, exhibitions, and seminars on development issues since 1988.

Even though 500 Japanese local authorities are involved in twinning, only a few have ties with the South. Hyogo Prefecture has been working with the Parana State in Brazil since 1970 by sending municipal staff and corporate technicians to Brazil and (after 1983) by setting up a center for industrial technology in Parana. The Hiroshima Prefecture has been training and providing experts and information to Szechwan Province in China in the fields of commerce, science and technology, and agriculture, and training Chinese university students. Osaka's link with Shanghai led to a collaboration to reduce Shanghai's air pollution and develop its port.

Since 1982, the city of Yokohama has played an instrumental role in developing Asia Pacific Citynet, a network of 17 cities (including Jakarta, Manila, Hanoi, Shanghai, Seoul, and Nagoya). Citynet has sponsored more than a dozen projects, including a workshop on how to build a million new housing units for the poor in Sri Lanka.

The flow of assistance in Japanese linkings has generally been North to South, but one exception has been the relationship between the Japanese rural mountain village of Toga with the Nepali village of Tukche. Toga hosted a famous mandala painter from Tukche for 18 months and is now building a meditation hall which will house the paintings completed during his stay.

Generally, Japanese linkings have not embraced development education. In fact, it is questionable whether linkings have facilitated increased cultural understanding at all, because few of the Japanese participants in these exchanges can converse comfortably in a foreign language.

Evaluation of Japanese CDIs is difficult, in part because there have been so few of them. The general consensus is that they have not had a significant impact on the population. Most Japanese communities have yet to understand why they should be involved in CDIs, and most NGOs have yet to be persuaded of the benefits of joint action with local governments.

To draw greater public interest in the Cologne Appeal, Community Link International, a Japanese NGO, sponsored visits by the founders of Towns and Development in 1987, 1988, and 1991. In 1989 the Japan International Co-operation Agency (JICA) established a committee of local government officials, university professors, and consultants to evaluate and stimulate CDIs. This committee published a report in early 1991, but it has not yet drawn up a concrete plan to implement its recommendations. Meanwhile, several recent events have increased Japanese interest in CDIs: growing national debate over decentralizing authority in the country; the election of a new Prime Minister, Morihiro Hosokawa, whose manifesto endorses people-centered development; the beginning of a program, under the leadership of Sister Cities International in the United States, to link US–Japanese sisters with partners in the South and the East; and a spate of CDI conferences and articles throughout Japan.

Kenya

Today, nearly thirty years after breaking away from British colonial rule, the majority of Kenyans live in abject poverty. Four out of five live in rural areas where roads, railways, electricity, and telephones are either absent or in total disrepair.

A key institution for mobilizing Kenyans for the formidable tasks of development has been local government. One hundred and four local authorities are members of the Association of Local Government Authorities of Kenya (ALGAK), and all but two are run by popularly elected councils. Generally local authorities in both urban and rural areas play an important role in building roads and schools, installing electricity and telephone lines, and providing affordable housing. But municipal governments are finding themselves less and less able to cope with burgeoning problems of migration, slums, unemployment, prostitution, drugs, and street violence. One reason local governments are failing is that they resist recognizing the single largest employer in the country: the informal sector.

The social and economic gaps left by national and local officials have been filled by 400 NGOs. These organizations promote sustainable development by educating and mobilizing people, by transferring technology, by launching small-scale business enterprises, and by setting up pilot projects on everything from community-based health care to family planning. NGOs are responsible for 40 percent of the health-care services in the country (up to 80 percent in rural areas) and 45 percent of the vocational training. Closely allied with NGOs are numerous community groups, of which an estimated 30,000 are women's self-help groups.

Recognizing the significance of NGOs in Kenya's development, Northern development agencies cover about a quarter of their total budgets. Foreign contributions to Kenyan NGOs in 1985 were $1.1 billion, with the biggest contributors being the EC and the Canadian International Development Agency.

In 1990 representatives of Kenya's local governments, NGOs, and community groups founded the Kenya One World Linking Forum to follow, evaluate, and promote North–South linkings and twinnings. The Forum tries to ensure that North–South partnerships are devoid of paternalism and exploitation. It encourages exchange programs to involve local officials, city administrators, young people, women leaders, cultural groups, schools, churches, and sports teams in which both Northern and Southern participants can learn and grow.

An example of a successful twinning partnership is that between Kisumu, the third largest city in Kenya, and Cheltenham in the United Kingdom. The relationship began when an Englishman named Dennis Mitchell met Philemon Amadi, a Kenyan studying in Cheltenham. After learning about Kisumu from Amadi, Mitchell traveled to Kisumu to explore the possibility of setting up a link. Cecilia Obuya from Kisumu then visited Cheltenham for three months. Obuya's trip coincided with Towns and Development's conference in Cologne, which inspired her to write a report entitled "An African View of Cheltenham." The twinning relationship was formalized shortly thereafter and facilitated two-way youth exchanges. Since then, Kisumu has also become a sister city of Roanoke, Virginia, in the United States. Thanks to its twinning, Kisumu's vocational teachers received 51 used typewriters and its municipal officers were able to attend technical training courses.

Linkings with Kenyan schools have also been popular. An example is the relationship between the Wallingford School in the United Kingdom and the Machakos Boys and Girls High Schools in Kenya. The headmaster of Wallingford suggested the link when two Kenyans were studying at Bristol University. Within a year students and teachers from the two schools were exchanging letters, photographs, and teaching materials. The objectives included learning about each other, creating bonds of friendship, conveying more positive images of Africa, and opening up other exchanges. By and large, these objectives were met – with one exception: Wallingford students and teachers have visited Kenya, but thus far no Machakos students and teachers have been able to afford a trip north.

Because of the importance of NGOs in Kenya, many Northerners work with them exclusively and avoid Kenyan local authorities. Northern donor agencies, for example, contribute to a Kenyan NGO called the Undugu Society, which gives food, shelter, clothing, and comfort to impoverished children roaming the slums of Nairobi who are known as "parking boys." Undugu Friends Circles in Germany and Holland make cash donations and periodically visit their Kenyan partners. The Kenyan government and many international donors also support the Kenya Energy and Environment Association (Kengo), which promotes the spread of renewable energy technologies.

While some members of the Kenya One World Linking Forum seem satisfied with the current assortment of CDIs, others are critical. First, with so much emphasis on the North providing aid and material gifts to Kenyans, linking and twinning relations have been imbalanced. Some Kenyans believe they must be more imaginative in coming up with an agenda of mutual learning unrelated to material gain, one that enables Kenyans to share their political, social, ethical, cultural, religious, and intellectual assets with their linking partners. Second, the initiative for linking and twinning has come almost exclusively from the North. Kenyans themselves must play a more active role in launching CDIs. Third, linking and twinning relationships have been virtually monopolized by a small number of Kenyan local officials. The structures overseeing the country's linking and twinning programs – including that of local governments themselves – must become more democratic and accountable. Finally, new ways must be found to motivate Kenyans to volunteer for CDI programs, because most communities cannot afford paid staff.

Netherlands

With more than twenty years of experience, NGOs and local authorities in the Netherlands have implemented an impressive array of CDIs. Of the 650 municipalities in the country, 430 are involved in some form of development cooperation, 250 have ties (or soon will have ties) with the countries of Central and Eastern Europe, and 80 are (or were) campaigning against apartheid in South Africa.

Surveys of Dutch CDIs have revealed that most of the larger cities in the country are active in several different fields. The 40 Dutch cities with more than 60,000 inhabitants all participate in North–South development cooperation and three-quarters have links with the East. Some of these larger municipalities also have prepared policy papers on "local global policy."

Dutch CDIs began in 1969, when the General Assembly of the United Nations proclaimed the 1970s the "second decade of development." Dozens of Dutch municipalities supported the UN campaign by educating the public or contributing financial resources to the South. Provincial executives, however, refused to allow the donations. The president of the Association of Netherlands Municipalities (VNG) responded by arguing that the national government could not hope to influence public opinion on North–South issues if the political bodies closest to the people were shut out of the debate.

This argument seemed to carry the day. In 1972 the Dutch House of Parliament gave municipalities permission to involve themselves in development cooperation on two conditions: community residents had to be directly involved in the CDI, and the local initiatives could not interfere with the nation's foreign policy. Dutch communities met the first condition by giving grants to local development-oriented NGOs (some of which had international projects), and more or less adhered to the second (the exceptions are noted below).

The Ministry of Internal Affairs and Development Cooperation revised the law in 1976, requiring that "development aid should first and foremost be accompanied by concrete action from the municipal population." Community participation has indeed been a key characteristic of Dutch CDIs. Trade unions, professional associations, businesses, churches, universities, and all other walks of life are involved.

A key catalyst for Dutch CDIs was the government's decision, in the early 1970s, to establish the National Committee on Development Education (NCO), which provided more than 10 million guilders ($5.4 million) annually to NGOs involved in North–South development cooperation. It was not until 1980, however, that one of NCO's entrepreneurial officers, Paul van Tongeren, began to recruit town councils. By undertaking surveys, holding conferences, and sponsoring courses for council members and civil servants, NCO raised the visibility and legitimacy of CDIs. It also invested $1.5 million each year to co-finance 22 Development Education Centers around the country. In addition, the Dutch government created two other funds, each disbursing $1 million per year, to support CDIs; one finances trips of Dutch experts to towns in the South, and the other supports fund-raising and initiatives within the Netherlands such as public education.

The motives for Dutch communities to involve themselves in international affairs mirror those found elsewhere: the global nature of many problems and the need for global action to remedy them, the special skills held by localities, and the proximity of local authorities to the people. But there are some motivations for CDIs that are more uniquely Dutch. As a small nation long surrounded by powerful nations, the Netherlands has historically been an accommodator and peace-maker. Dependent on shipping and trade, the Dutch have maintained an internationalist, "mercantilist" outlook. A typical Dutch teenager graduating from high school knows three or four languages. And the deep roots of Calvinism nurture a widespread sense of responsibility for fellow human beings.

While the origins of specific CDIs vary, they usually begin with one or more community groups that wish to expand the reach of their international work. These groups put a proposal before the city council, which in turn prepares a broader analysis of all the community's international contacts. The municipality might then hold a public meeting, put together a policy plan, set up a working group involving both activists and local politicians, give an alderman responsibility for coordinating local activities, and create a CDI line item on the city budget.

The Dutch give development education very high priority, believing that a change in the attitudes and behavior of people in the North is necessary to solve the problems in the South. Communities educate the public on development issues through Third World shops, school curricula, leaflets, exhibitions, and "One World" weeks. Twenty-two Dutch cities have Development Education Centers which provide information and advice to groups involved in North–South issues.

About 250 Dutch communities are involved in linking, twinning, and project support. The earliest twinning relationships, often arranged hastily by city council members without much research or popular support, did not fare well. In the early 1980s, however, the principal development-oriented NGOs in Holland, such as SNV (the Dutch Volunteers Organization) and NOVIB (the Dutch equivalent of the British Oxfam), set up a "linking platform" to help municipalities choose partners more carefully. Roughly half the country's links were created this way. Communities provided NGOs with a list of their interests, and NGOs then found partners in the South who shared these interests (thus, for example, a Dutch fishing village might be paired with a fishing village in Nigeria).

Linking has provided a framework for other kinds of CDIs, especially development education, project support, and technical assistance. Waddinxveen's ties with Toma, Burkina Faso, and with Lima, Peru, stimulated community discussions on human rights, the debt crisis, apartheid, and environmental protection. Inspired by its links, the city in 1992 prepared a policy paper called "International Aspects," which laid the foundation for municipal support of Amnesty International, a Third World shop and East–West friendship links. A working group affiliated with the African and Latin American linking programs helped local elementary schools develop learning materials, courses, festivals, and a newspaper on development cooperation.

Dutch linking organizers have become increasingly interested in technical assistance. Delft joined forces with four other European cities to support a water project in Esteli, Nicaragua. The port authorities of Amsterdam and Helsinki teamed up to develop the harbor of Beira in Mozambique.

All these CDIs have been boosted by financing from many different sources, including city budgets. For over six years Amsterdam raised more than 5.5 million guilders ($3 million) for projects in Managua, and about a fifth of that total came from the city budget. Amsterdam demonstrated that once a city makes a strong financial commitment to CDIs, it is easier to secure matching donations from international organizations, national agencies, businesses, foundations, and private citizens.

Even though Dutch cities are not supposed to interfere with the foreign policy of the Netherlands, some have nevertheless lobbied national officials on controversial foreign-policy issues. In the early 1980s about a hundred Dutch local authorities protested NATO's deployment of the cruise and Pershing II intermediate-range missiles by declaring their communities "nuclear-free." A number of these cities urged national officials to cut the defense budget. These campaigns were often conducted alongside peace-education programs and twinnings with cities in the Warsaw Pact countries.

Sometimes the targets of Dutch campaigns have been officials of the European Community or the leaders of other countries. In 1988, when representatives of 150 European towns linked with Nicaragua gathered in Amsterdam, they appealed to the United States and the Soviet Union not to intervene militarily in Central America.

Some Dutch cities, as noted in Chapter 2, have used their purchasing and investing decisions to influence international affairs, though the legality of such actions remains uncertain. In 300 Dutch communities and in eleven out of twelve provinces, government staff are drinking Max Havelaar "solidary coffee" – coffee bought from small-scale producers in the South at a "fair" price. Eighty-four Dutch municipalities joined LOTA (Local Authorities Against Apartheid), which tried unsuccessfully to mount a municipal boycott against Royal Dutch Shell. Two-thirds of the communities in the Netherlands agreed to stop using tropical hardwoods in public projects, though once again the government ruled the acts illegal.

The spread of CDIs throughout the Netherlands has been facilitated not only by the national government, NCO, and the nation's development-oriented NGOs but also by all the main political parties and the VNG. In 1985 the VNG and NCO organized a conference where 400 participants (mostly mayors, aldermen, and council members) discussed CDIs. Now the VNG has three full-time and two part-time staff promoting North–South development cooperation and coordinating a network of 82 cities with municipal peace policies.

Dutch CDIs have remarkable breadth and depth. At a conference held at Soesterberg in 1989, the largest 40 cities in the country discussed their activities in the fields of development cooperation, peace promotion, and opposition to apartheid. All but one of the cities were active in development cooperation, 36 were active in at least two fields, and 26 were active in all three. A later survey revealed that 100 of the largest Dutch cities are spending annually on CDIs at least one guilder per capita or a total of 9 million guilders ($4.9 million). The question Dutch communities are now asking is not whether to implement CDIs but how to create more unified, coherent "municipal global policies."

Nicaragua

Nicaragua has received more attention from Northern communities than any other country in the South. According to Jan Willem Bertens, former ambassador of the Netherlands to Nicaragua, "Town twinning in...Nicaragua [is] a unique phenomenon in the sense that in recent history there have been no other examples of revolutions that have received such strong support on such a massive scale by means of town twinning."

During the 1980s North Americans and Europeans set up more than 400 sister cities and linkings with Nicaragua. Many Northerners were drawn to Nicaragua because, as Monica Baltodano, a Sandinista commandante, writes, it was "the first time a revolutionary movement, having taken power by armed force, had gone on to prepare and consolidate the path to democracy, to give real freedom and means of participation to other political forces which had real autonomy." Other Northerners, particularly Americans, felt compelled to come to the aid of the Sandinistas when they were under siege from the Reagan-supported contra rebels.

The Sandinistas regarded the solidarity movement as "decisive" for the survival of the Nicaraguan revolution. According to a "basic document" prepared by the party: "International solidarity prevented the isolation of Nicaragua at the moments of greatest confrontation against North American aggression. It constituted one of the most important obstacles to greater levels of intervention, including direct invasion." The document further noted that the solidarity movement "compensated for the blocking of sources of finance from multilateral organizations and aid programmes." Finally, because the movement drew the attention of international media, it "played a crucial role in the revelation and denunciation of the events which took place in our country."

The Managua-based Popol Na Foundation for Promotion of Municipal Development recently surveyed 31 Nicaraguan communities from five of the nine regions in the country. These communities had a total of 138 twinning relationships with the North: 22 formed during the first four years of the San-dinistas' rule; 52 between 1984 and 1986, during the height of the contra war; and 63 between 1987 and 1990.

Periodic conferences in the North helped to strengthen and spread these twinnings, as did the establishment of the Information Center for Europe–Nicaragua Twinning, funded in part by the EC. The Nicaraguan government also assisted twinnings through regulations, policies, and institutions that allowed foreign visitors and goods to enter the country more easily.

Compared to their American counterparts, European linking partners came with more official support from local authorities and more financial aid. While the European partners tended to have specialized skills in education, health, and ecology, American partners tended to be citizen activists representing religious groups, veterans' organizations, trade unions, and universities. Both American and European participants were interested in informing their publics back home about Nicaragua and in establishing personal contact with Nicaraguans. The Europeans were more supportive of the Sandinistas and more interested in development cooperation in general, while the Americans focused on people-to-people relationships. By and large the Nicaraguans supported all these objectives.

The Popol Na Foundation survey found that the 138 twinning ties involved 457 "transactions:" 154 cash donations, 183 donations of material goods, 85 work brigades, and 85 other kinds of transactions. Cash donations were $7 million and material goods donations were worth $6.5 million. Roughly half the projects were financed by solidarity committees, a third by town councils, and a fifth through national co-financing.

Where were these transactions targeted? On the basis of the number of trans-actions, most were directed at the educational sector (24 percent), municipal projects (16 percent), or the health sector (15 percent). On the basis of the value of the transactions, the leading targets were municipal projects ($4.1 million), water projects ($3.1 million), education ($2.1 million), and health care ($2.1 million). These investments comprised on average half of *all* municipal investment in the towns studied, and 90 percent in some poor towns.

Twinning participants faced numerous obstacles throughout the 1980s. Com-munication within Nicaragua and between partners was difficult. Many Nicaraguan communities could be reached only after long, arduous drives. Long delays were common. Since most of the Nicaraguans running local authorities had no previous experience with administration and little formal education, Americans and Europeans found that they had no qualified counterparts for many projects. The absence of financial, technical, or human resources made the completion of projects difficult. And on top of all of these problems were the US-imposed embargo and the ever-present danger of being attacked by the contras.

Following the Sandinistas' loss of the national elections in 1990, the Nicaraguan government's support for twinning declined precipitously. Of the 138 twinnings surveyed, 69 received government assistance between 1980 and 1990, but only 16 did after 1990. The government decided no longer to waive customs duties for sister-city participants, simplify immigration procedures, or assist with the transportation of equipment and containers. Many projects are now stagnating.

Respondents to the Popol Na Foundation survey said that the main achievements of twinnings were to provide solidarity and to inform the North of the real state of affairs in Nicaragua. People on both sides also noted that twinning reduced Nicaragua's isolation, counteracted misinformation, heightened Northern awareness of conditions in the South, and alleviated some of the suffering caused by the embargo. Using their twinning ties, solidarity groups were also able to monitor national elections in 1984 and 1990.

What do Nicaraguans want to happen next with their twinnings? Survey respondents made the following recommendations.

- To ensure continuity of sister-city programs, institutions should be formed within Nicaraguan municipalities that are outside the control of local government.
- Northern solidarity groups should continue working with Nicaraguan counterparts to provide further aid, to complete unfinished projects, to strengthen local democracy, and to secure the current state of peace.
- Whenever one Nicaraguan town is twinned with more than one community in the North, Northern partners should try to coordinate their work.
- The successes of the Nicaraguan twinning movement should be communicated to a broader audience both in the North and within Nicaragua.
- Northern partners should try to improve the administrative know-how of municipalities in Nicaragua and provide them with appropriate technology.
- Existing twinnings should be strengthened through more linkings and more North–South–East relationships.

Norway

CDIs in Norway come from a long Nordic tradition of helping others. For many years NORAD (the Norwegian government agency of development), the Norwegian volunteer organization, and Kirkens Nodhjelp (the Norwegian church-aid organization), along with a number of other Norwegian NGOs, provided aid and performed missionary work in the South. Over time, however, a more sophisticated view of North–South relations began to take hold, one which followed the main points of the Cologne Appeal. There are currently 35 links between Norwegian communities and the South. In Norway the terms "friendship-group" (*vennebygruppe*) and "friendship-cooperation" (*vennskapssamarbeid*) have been used to describe these links. (There is no other good translation of the words "twinning" or "linking" in Norwegian.)

After Guatemala experienced a devastating earthquake in 1976, a member of the Kirkens Nodhjelp team that assisted with the clean-up, Petter Skauen, decided to use his contacts with the Mayan Indians to set up two Norway–Guatemala links: one between Fredrikstad and San Martin (established in 1986), and another between Krakeroy and the small mountain village of Patzun (established in 1988). These ties grew to include football players, teachers, housewives, politicians, bakers, nursery-school students, and trade unionists. By focusing Norwegian public attention on the well-being of Patzun residents, Krakeroy helped deter death squads and the Guatemalan army from harassing their partners.

Fredrikstad's link with San Martin began in 1984 when firemen in the two towns corresponded and has since emphasized solidarity and aid. Fredrikstad managed to raise 50,000 kroner ($7,700) per year to improve San Martin's water supply. Funds for this and other projects were disbursed through the local staff of Kirkens Nodhjelp in Guatemala.

The starting point for Kristiansand's link with Rajshahi, Bangladesh, was a massive Norwegian aid program in the early 1970s. With funds raised from Kristiansand's schools and cultural events, partners in Rajshahi were able to dig water wells, to educate nurses, and to equip a health clinic. But the initial emphasis on aid was problematic; when the key fund-raisers in the North lost interest, the program ground to a halt. Today, friendship committees on both sides emphasize citizen involvement.

The residents of Hof have related to their partners in Rifiji, Tanzania, primarily as pen-pals, with Norwegian volunteers in Tanzania translating letters into Swahili and the replies from Rifiji into Norwegian. The system had some start-up problems, because volunteers were expected to do the translating on top of their regular work. This, along with the frequent turnover of volunteers in Tanzania, meant long delays between messages.

Stavanger has linked with politically controversial partners: Esteli in Nicaragua, Antsirabe in Madagascar, and Nablus on the West Bank. Directed by an executive secretary and financially supported by the city's Recreational Office, these "solidarity" twinnings involve 22 discrete groups within the community, including nursery schools and trade unions. In Stavanger, as in Kristiansand, Fredrikstad, and Krakeroy, the city council has been directly involved. This means that politicians and citizens, along with local NGOs and grassroots movements, take part in the day-to-day administration of the programs.

Verdal's relationship with a displaced group of black South Africans in Tanzania also is politically interesting. In a written agreement with its partners, Verdal pledged to distribute information about South Africa in Norway and to raise funds to help the refugees' children attend the Solomon Mahlanga Freedom College in Tanzania. Verdal's creative fund-raising events have included sales of second-hand objects and an exhibition of drawings.

Regular visits have been the central element of Sauda's link with San Juan del Sur in Nicaragua. The Nicaraguans coming to Sauda have found themselves honored at concerts or children's art exhibitions. Sauda also raised funds to purchase school materials, a church bell, and a nursery school for its Nicaraguan partners. As in the case of Stavanger, nearly two dozen different groups within the city are linked with Nicaraguan counterparts.

Suldal established a link with the Nepali villages of Urma and Urmi in 1989. Suldal residents visited Nepal and then prepared exhibitions and slide-shows to raise Norwegian awareness about Nepal. The link has been hampered by limited language skills on both sides and the poor postal system in Nepal.

A number of Norwegian links – including Nadderud's with India, Greaker's with El Salvador, Bryn's with Gambia, and Oppegard's with Bangladesh – have involved children (see Chapter 2 for details.) The Greverud School in Oppegard holds a weekly cafe to raise money for projects benefiting children in Thanapara, Bangladesh. These funds – totalling 10,000 kroner ($1,500) in 1990 – support preventative health care, acute medical treatment, purchases of school materials, and courses on gardening. Children in Oppegard and Thanapara also write to one another and exchange drawings.

Risor's ties with Sutukoba, a small village in Gambia, began when two Gambian students enrolled in Risor Technical College. The residents of Risor decided to help their partners by sending clothing and money. Inspired by the generosity of their Norwegian friends, young people in Sutukoba formed a soccer club called the "Helga team" and a youth organization which, among other things, cleans the streets and takes care of the sick and the elderly. Two other community groups in Risor helped 420 women in Sutukoba acquire plots of land to grow their own food.

Through a television show entitled "Women of the Third World," the community of Nesodden raised 1.2 million kroner ($190,000) to help educate poor women in Dinajpur district of Bangladesh. The aid program, however, required so much energy that the other aspects of the linking program died from inattention. People-to-people contact is slowly being reestablished.

A full-time secretary working for Friendship North–South (Vennskap Nord/Sor), which is administered as part of the Norwegian Ex-volunteer Association (Fredskorpssambandet), coordinates Norway's linking network. Kirkens Nodhjelp also has one person working full-time on CDIs.

Philippines

CDIs in the Philippines, despite major obstacles, are gradually becoming part of the Filipino people's struggle to improve their living conditions and to create self-reliant local economies. The need for a new approach to development in the country is clear. Seven out of ten Filipinos live below the poverty line, and the income gap between rich and poor is widening. To help repay its enormous international debt, the government has allowed loggers and agribusiness to clear away 8 million hectares of prime forest over the last 15 years. At the same time the country's food supply has declined, and soil erosion, siltation, and sedimentation have destroyed farmlands, fishing grounds, and fresh water sources.

Filipino NGOs are skeptical of the term "community development." As far back as the 1950s, the Philippines responded to the country's emerging economic problems by teaming up with the United States to promote "community development" through the Presidential Assistance on Community Development (PACD), the forerunner of the present Department of the Interior and Local Government (DILG). The main funds for this program came from the US Central Intelligence Agency and US Agency for International Development (AID). In other words, development assistance at the local level was closely linked with US covert action and counter-insurgency activities. Operation Brotherhood, for example, which was supposed to be providing "socio-medical" services to resettle slum dwellers, was actually training personnel for CIA work in Laos and Vietnam. The NGOs involved in these official assistance efforts tended to be affiliated with foreign humanitarian and evangelical institutions, many of which covertly supported the US government's low-intensity conflict (LIC) program. From the outset, these NGOs viewed themselves as carrying out government policies. By the 1970s, NGOs looking at the fundamental causes of underdevelopment concluded that the government's programs were not meeting the needs of the people. They decided to organize mass movements and to promote "social consciousness based on the existing conflict of class interests."

As NGOs became more militant, the US-backed dictatorship of Ferdinand Marcos fought back. Development workers who were creating new organizations and new socio-economic projects became the targets of government anti-insurgency operations; many were killed. This only deepened the commitment of Filipino NGOs to form what became known as "cause-oriented groups."

Despite this history, a few development-oriented NGOs collaborated successfully with the government. One example is the Area-Based Child Survival and Development Programme (ABCSDP), which was supported by the Philippines government and by UNICEF. After a poor start in 1987, ABCSDP recruited the International Institute of Rural Reconstruction to deliver health and nutrition services to municipalities in Negros Occidental through youth clubs, farmers' cooperatives, and women's groups.

Other joint NGO-government endeavors, however, have not fared as well. With financial support from the German Federal Ministry for Economic Cooperation (BMZ), the Philippines government started a project on the Bondoc Peninsula, where 155 landlords own nearly all the coconut plantations and where 80 percent of the population can barely survive on their wages as tenants. Officially the project was aimed at "improvements in agricultural productivity and marketing, provision of public services like education and health, and more efficient management of local resources and the environment," but 80 percent of the project's $19 million in funds were earmarked for new roads. The German Agency for Technical Cooperation (GTZ) agreed to work with grassroots groups, but the contracts it sent to local NGOs for signature limited their participation to being consultants. The NGOs were furious. They feared that their cooperation would be used to legitimate a project that would do little for the poor. Unlike the government, the NGOs were convinced that the only way to alleviate poverty was to redistribute land. While an official German mission in 1989 recommended proceeding only if it promoted agrarian reform, human rights, and grassroots participation, the GTZ nevertheless decided to push ahead with the project as originally conceived.

This example shows that many factors have to be considered for a partnership between government agencies and NGOs (or a partnership between Southern and Northern groups) to succeed. Many NGOs remain hopeful that constructive joint action with local governments might be possible in the future. One good sign is that in 1991 the Local Government Code was revised to give local authorities in the Philippines greater power and autonomy vis-à-vis the national government.

Spain

Even though Spain was considered a developing country by the World Bank and the International Monetary Fund until 1980, it actually became an international donor in 1977. The entry of Spain into the European Community in 1986 marked the beginning of new commitments in North–South development cooperation, including those undertaken by municipalities.

Spanish CDIs arose from several different sources. As a Catholic colonial power with a history of missionary work, Spain has long had an interest in the South, particularly in Latin America. After the overthrow of General Francisco Franco, Spaniards interested in assisting the South were motivated less by missionary zeal and more by "solidarity" with the poor. Many also felt an ethical duty to help countries in Latin America which, like their own, were trying to democratize and strengthen civil society.

FEMP, the national Federation of Municipalities, was founded in 1981 to develop Spanish communities, and it was not much of a stretch for FEMP to take an interest in the development of communities outside the country. From the outset, FEMP and Spanish municipalities looked to NGOs with international expertise to help them formulate CDIs. The one exception to this pattern was the transfer of urban technology to the South, an area in which municipalities regarded themselves as having the greatest expertise.

Several international organizations have supported CDIs in Spain. Three are based in Europe: the World Federation of United Cities (FMCU), the International Union of Local Authorities (IULA), and the Council of European Municipalities and Regions (CEMR). Two others are based in Latin America: the Latin-American Organization of Intermunicipal Cooperation (OICI) and the Union of Latin-American Capital Cities (UCCI).

Spanish CDIs have not challenged national policies, in part because the national government provides substantial funding to NGOs most active in North–South issues. Development-oriented NGOs even signed an agreement on program guidelines with AECI (the Spanish Agency of International Cooperation, which is part of Spain's Foreign Office) in 1990. But the strong involvement of the national government has not undercut the responsiveness of these NGOS to public demands to ship food to Africa, to stop the civil wars in Central America, and to promote global ecological protection.

The first contacts between local governments and NGOs occurred at the "Conference on Hunger in the World," held in Madrid in January 1986. The city council of Madrid, then under the leadership of Enrique Tierno Galvan, co-sponsored the conference, and an NGO called IEPALA presented 40 projects for possible joint action.

CDIs, however, remained rare until 1988, when local governments began to allocate money to twinnings. Several conferences enabled NGOs and local authorities to become better acquainted: the First Workshop on Cooperation for Development, held at Valladolid in April 1989; the Meeting between Local Corporations and NGOs for Development, held at Vitoria-Gazteiz in October 1990; and the First Basque Municipal Meeting for International Cooperation, held in October 1992. In October 1991 the Foreign Office and the State Secretariat for International Cooperation also published a leaflet on possibilities for NGO cooperation with local authorities.

In a survey released by the International Department of FEMP in September 1990, more than half the responding communities reported that they had sponsored development-related "exhibitions and cultural activities." One out of two had made "economic contributions for political and humanitarian solidarity campaigns," which included everything from solidarity work in Chile to disaster relief. A smaller number of respondents said they had sponsored development-oriented conferences (45 percent), financed projects in the South (24 percent), and provided training for Latin American technicians or politicians (23 percent).

Spanish communities have supported a wide range of projects in Latin America. Lekeitio set up fishing projects in Nicaragua and Uruguay. In partnership with the NGO IPADE, the city of Valencia contributed 6.3 million pesetas ($61,300) for a pilot project in Managua to provide drinking water and to recycle polystyrene. Valencia also joined with the NGO Manos Unidas to invest 3.1 million pesetas ($30,200) in septic tanks and water filters for the municipality of Sao Joao dos Patos in Brazil.

Many local governments demanded an official framework for CDIs. In 1991 FEMP and AECI responded by signing a general agreement spelling out what localities could and could not do in the field of development cooperation. They also created mechanisms through which the national government and localities could consult with one another and exchange information. And they committed themselves to publishing an annual "Plan of International Cooperation," financed with 7.2 million pesetas ($70,000) from FEMP and 5.8 million pesetas ($56,000) from AECI.

FEMP's 1990 survey revealed that only 17 percent of the municipalities in Spain had *not* undertaken CDIs. Nearly half had been involved in four activities, a quarter in three activities, and a sixth in one activity. Nearly all of the localities sampled (83 percent) had been involved in public education on North-South "solidarity and sensitization."

Twinnings often provided an important framework for other CDIs. Roughly half of the municipalities twinned with Southern communities exchanged technical information or brought technical experts or politicians from their partner communities to Spain for training (11 percent of Spanish communities without twins also trained people from the South). Another interesting finding was that 76 percent of the municipalities with twinnings were involved in "solidarity and sensitization," compared to 31 percent of municipalities without twinnings.

The FEMP study revealed that the participation of NGOs in twinning activities has been quite limited. Nevertheless, a few noteworthy examples of joint action have occurred. An NGO called the Catalonian Fund for Cooperation for Development enlisted the help of 135 Catalonian city councils. The Basque Fund for Cooperation with Central America received widespread support from Spanish Basque communities, especially Vitoria-Gazteiz, which had sponsored the First Basque Municipal Meeting for International Cooperation.

There have been surprisingly few CDIs to protect the environment. Municipalities have tried to manage environmental problems on their own, and generally favored economic development over environmental protection.

In the fields of peace and human rights, NGOs have been more active than municipalities. But a few communities have been active in these more contentious areas. Barcelona and Hospitalet set up peace-information centers, subsidized peace-oriented NGOs, prepared peace-education materials for the schools, and renamed streets for the "Mothers of the Plaza de Mayo," "Gandhi," and "Olaf Palme."

Several CDIs are focusing on the needs of women. The Spanish government's "Plan of Action," which includes suggested actions for local authorities and NGOs, has provisions calling for international cooperation on women's issues. Many of the local governments run by the Socialist Party have Councilor Boards of Women that contribute to international programs. And FEMP itself has a Commission for Women that works internationally.

Perhaps the most significant promoter of CDIs has been IEPALA, which maintains close ties with both NGOs and local authorities in the field. In collaboration with the UCCI, IEPALA has trained 300 mayors, town councilors, and municipal staff from Latin America.

United Kingdom

For the past 30 years NGOs have been raising public awareness on "Third World issues" in the United Kingdom. The World Development Movement campaigned on North–South issues in the 1960s and was joined in the 1970s and 1980s by the more established organizations such as Oxfam, Christian Aid, War on Want, and the Catholic Fund for Overseas Development. While the Labour Party was in power, the UK government also funded Development Education Centres (DECs).

With only a few exceptions, local governments did not really get involved with development cooperation until 1980, when two important events occurred. One was the first free election in Zimbabwe. Several chief executives of British local authorities who went to Zimbabwe to help supervise the election returned with a commitment to assist their African counterparts. The second event was publication of the Brandt Commission report, which ex-Prime Minister Edward Heath cited when he told a national twinning conference in 1983 that local governments should press for changing the North–South balance.

By 1992, 36 UK communities were formally twinned with Southern partners and another 116 had informal linking ties. Roughly half of the local authorities in the country were undertaking one kind of CDI or another, and these were supplemented by numerous North–South links involving youth groups, schools, and universities. The Commonwealth Youth Exchange Council played a particularly important role in promoting these partnerships.

Four kinds of factors helped to stimulate and spread CDIs in the United Kingdom. One was a spirited public dialogue on North–South interdependence and on people-to-people links. Many British citizens questioned how their donations to large charities were being used and decided that direct personal aid would be more effective. The globally broadcast Band Aid concert raised awareness about famine in Ethiopia in 1984. And the growth of the environmental movement and publication of the Brundtland Commission report drew further public attention.

Political factors were also important. Twinnings, particularly twinnings with other European cities, became popular after World War Two as instruments of reconciliation and peace. Public concerns over apartheid, the nuclear arms race, and the contra war in Nicaragua led to some highly visible CDIs in the 1980s. By 1985, two-thirds of the population of England, Scotland, and Wales lived in a local jurisdiction that had some form of anti-apartheid policy, despite decrees from the central government prohibiting municipal sanctions. Over 170 local authorities declared themselves nuclear-free zones and challenged Prime

Minister Thatcher's defense policies by engaging in peace education, issuing reports on the consequences of nuclear war, and forming town twinnings with the Soviet Union and Eastern Europe. Oxford, Lambeth, and other cities set up ties with Nicaragua. The political mainstream and the Fleet Street press dismissed these CDIs as machinations of the "loony left," and even some linking organizers tried to distance themselves from these activist initiatives. But many controversial CDIs continue to this day. A number of the linkages with Nicaragua, for example, remain in place (despite the defeat of the Sandinistas at the polls in 1990).

Then there have been economic factors. The opening of Chinese trade with the West was followed by a burst of interest by UK cities in twinning with Chinese cities. More recently, UK cities have used linking as a way to establish trade relations with communities in Eastern and Central Europe.

A final factor heightening public interest in linking has been demography. Communities such as Gloucester, St Albans, Hackney (London), and Rochdale have seen linking, especially with the countries of origin for their own ethnic populations, as a way to improve local race relations.

Several organizations have been responsible for spreading CDIs. Starting in 1982, Oxfam-UK dedicated a part-time staff member to advise linking partners about good practice. But "promotion of linking," writes Jane Knight, Oxfam's linking liaison between 1985 and 1992, "was never encouraged, because there were seen to be too many risks of bad practice and perhaps harmful effects judged by current development thinking." (Oxfam recently terminated its linking post for budgetary reasons.)

In 1984 the linking movement had grown large enough to warrant the creation of the United Kingdom One World Linking Association (UKOWLA). Led by various full-time and part-time "professionals," UKOWLA brought Southerners to the United Kingdom so that they could speak for themselves in Northern forums.

Another organization helping Oxfam and UKOWLA with linking was the Local Government International Bureau (LGIB), which served as a conduit between UK local governments and international organizations such as the International Union of Local Authorities (IULA) and the Council of European Municipalities and Regions (CEMR). In 1990 the LGIB received enough funds from the British Overseas Development Administration (ODA) to create a developing-countries section with three committees: coordination, linking and cooperation, and education. Using its connections with many UK government agencies, the LGIB then helped local authorities set the nation's agenda for UNCED, prepare North–South technical training programs, and design national development-education programs. The LGIB's committee on linking commissioned a handbook for both Northerners and Southerners on *Preparing for Visits Overseas*, which was jointly written by Peter Batty and the late Musa Njiru from Kenya.

The Council of Europe's North–South Campaign brought together UK NGOs, local authorities, parliamentarians, and national officials for discussions on development cooperation in what became known as the "quadrilogue." This stimulated local authority interest and involvement in the 1988 Council of Europe Campaign and in the 1992 "One World" media campaign. The quadrilogue's agenda now is to mobilize local authorities and NGOs to implement Agenda 21 (from UNCED) at the community level.

Two additional points about UK CDIs are worth noting. First, from 1989 onwards they have involved Southern representatives. Second, women have played a leading role, despite male dominance in the local-authority world.

The main categories of CDI work in the United Kingdom are public information, development education, linking, campaigning, and project support.

Communities have used many techniques to spread information about development. The Cumbria County Council put on an exhibition about linking at its public libraries and schools. Sheffield, Bassetlaw, and Aberdeen used their town newspapers to publicize North–South activities. Cheltenham (which is linked with Kisumu, Kenya) and Bishopston (which is linked with KV Kuppam, India) decided that an effective way to spread information would be to open up Third World shops to sell products made by their linking partners.

Four major NGOs and a network of Development Education Centres (DECs) around the country assist local authorities with their development-education work. Birmingham, with support from its local DEC and from Oxfam, has organized educational tours to developing countries for its teachers and education officers. The local authority of Reading helps underwrite the neighborhood DEC. Two national policy papers boosted the legitimacy of development education by urging local educational authorities to integrate international perspectives into the school curriculum.

Thanks in part to the spread of the Cologne Appeal, linking has become perhaps the most significant CDI in the United Kingdom. The UK approach has been to emphasize long-term personal relationships leading to aid and joint problem-solving. A variety of NGOs, especially churches, have supported friendship links. Several examples suggest the range of linking experiences in the United Kingdom.

After the city of Warwick held a "One World Week" in 1979, it began to search for other ways to reach out to the South. Jane Knight, a resident of Warwick, writes:

> Our basic aim was to offer friendship to the Bo people [of Sierra Leone] so that we would have a more real, and not just academic knowledge of each other, and we in the Warwick district would use that knowledge to lobby our government more effectively for change in trade, aid, and debt policies.

Gradually the relationship grew to include links with a hospital, a library, and 16 schools. It also enabled the Bo people to make home visits and to study in Warwick. A side-effect of the program has been that Sierra Leoneans living in London were inspired to form stronger links with their homeland.

Several people in Marlborough were moved by the Brandt Commission report to set up a relationship with Gunjur in the Gambia in the early 1980s. Their initial ideas for action included educating the public and putting pressure on local politicians to address the North–South imbalance; the giving of aid was deliberately excluded. Members of the community were surprised, however, when their partners in Gunjur still requested funds to build an extention on to a school. The Marlborough linking partners turned down the request. Six months later, the Gambians asked again for help, this time providing documentation that 500 children in Gunjur were being educated in a building made out of banana leaves and bamboo which frequently collapsed. The Marlborough group called for a public debate on the question, and after a lively meeting that drew 120 people the community decided to provide the requested assistance. A builder and a group of young people from Marlborough worked alongside Gunjur residents to construct the classrooms. The following year 15 young people from Gunjur came to Marlborough to set up a playground on a council estate.

More recently residents of Marlborough have traveled to Gunjur to teach, to set up a plantation for mango and paw-paw trees, to build a library and pre-school center, and to donate a milling machine. Young people from Gunjur have come to Marlborough to learn trades such as welding and carpentry and to study at the British schools. Marlborough also has set up a DEC on a site provided by its education authority.

The multiracial composition of the London Borough of Hackney led to twinning relationships with France, Israel, Germany, Barbados, and South Africa. This last twinning tie, which is with the Alexandra Civic Association, began in 1986 as a gesture of solidarity. Today Hackney is providing technical training for Alexandrans so that they can run their local government more effectively.

NGOs have recruited local officials to participate in various campaigns. Many UK mayors marched in the 1987 "Walk for the World," which raised public awareness on North–South issues prior to the general election. UNCED increased the interest of UK local officials in global environment protection, particularly the prevention of global warming.

Finally, UK local authorities have supported many projects in the South, typically through fund-raising. Stevenage sent a fire-engine to Kadoma in Zimbabwe as part of a linking relationship between their fire departments. Staffordshire provided technical assistance to Accra in Ghana with World Bank funding, and is now trying to establish school linkings. One general problem with these CDIs, however, is that they rarely involve NGOs.

United States

CDIs in the United States emerged in two separate movements that may be converging. "Non-partisan" CDIs were promoted by organizations such as

Sister Cities International, the Partnership of the Americas, and the National League of Cities. Sister Cities International, the first and most active of these groups, has been responsible for creating more than 1,600 sister-city links in 96 countries – 619 of which are in the South. The second movement, which is politically progressive, is a loose network of activists and city council members who consider themselves the practitioners of "municipal foreign policy." Their principal work in the South has consisted of sanctions against South Africa, opposition to US military intervention in Latin America, and 100 sister communities with Nicaragua, El Salvador, and South Africa.

The roots of the non-partisan network go back to 1956, when President Dwight D. Eisenhower proposed that the United States set up a global network of twinned cities. "The sister-cities program is an important resource to the negotiations of governments in letting the people themselves give expression of their common desire for friendship, goodwill, and cooperation for a better world for all."

Fulfilling Eisenhower's vision, the National League of Cities linked US localities with their counterparts abroad and served as a clearing-house for these relationships. But as the number of sororal ties grew, so did the need for a new home. In 1967 the League's sister-cities work was transferred to a new organization called the Town Affiliation Association, and Sister Cities International (SCI) became its main project. Even though SCI is an non-governmental organization with a board composed of private citizens and local elected officials, it is chaired ceremonially by the President of the United States and supported by a modest annual grant from the US Information Agency (which in turn is overseen by the US State Department).

In 1977 SCI began to promote North–South development cooperation through its Emphasis Africa Program. Since then, the US Agency for International Development (AID) has given SCI a major grant each year to assist US cities interested in providing technical assistance to Southern partners. This work covers virtually all regions of the South and until recently was coordinated by one staff person, Peter Loan.

An organization similar to SCI is Partners of the Americas, which links US states with provinces or regions of countries in Latin America. Like SCI, Partners of the Americas has promoted cultural exchanges, joint projects, trade, and business development.

Both SCI and Partners of the Americas consider themselves "apolitical" and consequently have steered clear of controversial matters. Their objectives were friendship, good-will, and the economic advancement of the South. The strength of their approach was that the average, middle-of-the-road American felt comfortable participating in their work. But as more Americans became convinced that change in the United States was necessary for global development to succeed – particularly change in US foreign policy – a new approach emerged that became known as municipal foreign policy (MFP).

The MFP movement developed in the 1980s in opposition to the foreign policies of President Ronald Reagan. Its accomplishments were impressive:

- More than 800 local governments passed "nuclear-freeze" resolutions and helped pressure Reagan, the only modern US president to enter office on a platform condemning arms control, to launch the START negotiations in Geneva.
- By refusing to cooperate with the Federal Emergency Management Agency's "crisis relocation planning," more than 120 cities convinced the federal government to cancel its nuclear war civil defense program.
- By 1986, 65 cities and 19 states had divested more than $20 billion in pension funds out of corporations doing business in South Africa, persuading two-thirds of both houses of Congress to override a presidential veto and to replace Reagan's policy of "constructive engagement" with limited economic sanctions.
- Nearly ninety US sister cities with Nicaragua, flanked by thousands of grassroots activists, helped to keep American public opinion firmly against military support for the contras (in fact, this movement probably supplied more humanitarian assistance to the Nicaraguan people than all the military assistance Congress voted to the contras.)
- In 1989, at a time when Congress was dragging its feet on regulating chlorofluorocarbons (CFCs) and other chemicals threatening the protective ozone layer in the stratosphere, 27 US and Canadian cities met in Irvine, California, and resolved to begin banning these substances in their own jurisdictions; these cities ultimately pushed Congress to include the issue in the 1990 Clean Air Act.

Impressed by these successes, progressive activists and local elected officials set up two MFP networks dealing directly with development cooperation. One, which promoted sister cities with El Salvador (initially rebel-occupied areas), now has more than thirty communities participating. The second is a network of ten communities linked with civic associations in South Africa.

Different NGOs coordinated each of these MFP initiatives: the National Freeze Campaign (St Louis, Missouri) oversaw the nuclear-freeze movement; the Traprock Peace Center (Western Massachusetts) advocated non-participation in civil defense planning; TransAfrica (Washington, DC) and the American Committee on Africa (New York) coordinated the sanctions movement; the sister-city committees in Boulder, Madison, New Haven, Portland, Providence, and Seattle set up a network overseeing US–Nicaragua twinnings; the Center for Innovative Diplomacy (CID) in California (San Francisco and Irvine) launched the ozone-protection ordinances; New El Salvador Today (Baltimore) started the Salvadoran sister-cities movement (the network is now run by the National Center on US–El Salvador Sister Cities in New York); and the

US–South Africa Sister Community Project (San Francisco) promoted linking with the South African civics.

CID played a major role in networking all the MFP organizations by publishing the *Bulletin of Municipal Foreign Policy* for five years. In 1991 CID's environmental work was absorbed by the Toronto-based International Council for Local Environmental Initiatives (ICLEI), and the *Bulletin* was taken over by the Washington-based Institute for Policy Studies and published for another two years under the title *Global Communities*.

Relations between the MFP and non-partisan networks have never been smooth. The non-partisan organizers have feared that progressives would infect their work with a political agenda. MFP advocates worried that working with the non-partisan organizations would be tantamount to endorsing US foreign policy (and a few also worried that the non-partisan groups were associated with the US military and intelligence agencies.)

An example of the tensions between the two movements is evident in the early days of sister cities with the Soviet Union. President Richard Nixon's overtures to Communist Party Chair Leonid Brezhnev for détente were consummated in 1972 with the establishment of six US–Soviet sister cities. After the Soviet invasion of Afghanistan in 1979, however, détente collapsed and five of these sister cities were cancelled or abandoned. Hundreds of "citizen diplomacy" initiatives then began to challenge the renewed Cold War, and a dozen grassroots groups decided to set up new sister cities with the Soviet Union. Both the Soviet peace committees and SCI, afraid of challenging their respective governments, refused to help. So an independent network sprang up, promoted by two Floridians, Steve Kalishman of Gainesville and Bob Broedel of Tallahassee. As relations between the two countries began to improve in the mid-1980s, the mainstream organizations gradually took over the work of the independents – though tensions between the independent organizers and SCI still exist.

One way of understanding the differences between the non-partisan and MFP networks is to contrast their twinning activities. IPS and SCI recently surveyed cities with CDIs to compare programs affiliated with SCI with those of the "independents" (that is, communities twinned with Nicaragua, El Salvador, and South Africa). Sixty-seven cities completed the survey – 28 from SCI affiliates and 39 from the independents. What follows is a summary of the key findings:

1. *Most sister-city programs are quite small.* The average budget for all respondents is $10,000, and half have budgets lower than $4,500. Unlike European sister-city programs, which enjoy extensive support from local government, most US programs are funded by private contributions. Only 16 of the 67 respondents reported receiving even a penny from City Hall (13 SCI affiliates and three independents), and among these all but two received $5,000 or less. Four out of five US programs said they have no paid staff whatsoever, and most of the remaining programs have part-time staff. Only five programs have one or more

full-time staff. It is easy to see why all these programs depend heavily on volunteers.

Only a handful of programs have significant budgets (at least by European standards): New Haven–Leon (Nicaragua), which spends $100,000 per year; Seattle–Managua, which spends $60,000 per year; Palo Alto–Palo (Philippines), which spends $42,427 per year; and Cambridge–San Jose Las Flores (El Salvador), which spends $40,000 per year.

2. *The SCI affiliates and the independents are engaged in a diverse assortment of activities.* More than half the respondents hold events and distribute educational materials "on North–South issues or about [their] partner city," send and receive delegations, give "monetary aid in the form of grants," and provide in-kind assistance ("such as tools, medicine, books, etc."). About a third of those surveyed either "send technicians and other professions for on-site training" in their partner city or bring people from the partner city to their own "for technical training or education." Only four programs – Palo Alto (CA)–Palo; Amesbury (MA)–Esabalu (Kenya); New Haven (CT)–Leon; and Norwalk (CT)–Nagarote (Nicaragua) – said they were providing monetary aid in the form of "direct loans" or "a revolving loan fund (a grant that your partner uses to provide small loans)."

3. *SCI affiliates are more involved in business promotion than are the independents.* Generally, SCI affiliates see business promotion as a way that communities on both sides of the relationship can benefit, while the independents see it as serving the interests of only a few private entrepreneurs and not the interests of the communities as a whole. Two-thirds of SCI respondents call "promoting business relationships" a "very important" or "important" objective of their programs; two-thirds of the independents call business promotion "unimportant." It is not surprising that, according to the survey, nearly 80 percent of SCI affiliates are involved in business promotion, as contrasted to only 15 percent of the independents.

4. *SCI affiliates tend to work more closely with mainstream organizations than the independents do.* What institutions in the United States are "particularly helpful" for sister cities? At the local government level the SCI affiliates reported working closely with functional agencies such as the school system, the chamber of commerce, and the fire department. The independents, in contrast, said they work with the political organs of local government, namely the mayor and the city council.

With regard to non-governmental organizations (NGOs), the SCI affiliates reported that the following have been helpful: hospitals, trade centers, libraries, universities, community colleges, Lions Clubs, Rotary International chapters, and churches. (Interestingly, only two of the SCI programs mentioned Sister Cities International.) The independents said they work closely with three programs that have been most active in building national networks around their issue: the Wisconsin Coordinating Council on Nicaragua, the National Center for US–El Salvador Sister Cities, and the US–South African Sister Community

Project. Other NGOs mentioned by the independents were politically progressive organizations such as Quest for Peace, the Quixote Center, CISPES, SHARE, Technica, and the Pacifica radio stations.

5. *SCI affiliates encounter problems with bureaucracy, while the independents encounter problems with war and violence.* Because SCI requires its affiliates to follow certain protocols with foreign governments, every SCI respondent rated problems with bureaucracy as "significant" or "somewhat significant." A third of the independents, which often circumvent foreign governments altogether, reported no problems with bureaucracy.

Nearly two-thirds of SCI programs were unaffected by war or revolution, while three-quarters of the independents encountered problems with local violence. This is understandable given that the independents are all working in regions that have been embroiled in de facto civil wars.

6. *US sister-city programs have adopted a people-centered approach to development.* Well over 90 percent of the cities surveyed said that "improving mutual under-standing" and "developing long-term bonds of friendship" are "very important" or "somewhat important" goals. The importance sister cities place on providing partners with know-how was revealed in their answers to our questions about projects. Two out of three sister-city programs have "projects that support economic development in the partner city," such as digging water systems, setting up cooperatives, and building schools and hospitals. Three-quarters of the sister cities with projects deem it "very important" to "support projects that build self-reliance" and to "support projects that rely on local materials, local human resources, and appropriate technology."

7. *US sister-city programs have only begun to move from charity to justice.* Charitable aid remains a very large part of what US sister cities do. The 67 respondents reported that their cash contributions to partners in 1991 totaled $173,784, or about $2,600 per city. The respondents also sent an estimated $776,790-worth of in-kind assistance, or about $11,600 per city. Thus, US sister cities provide an average of $14,200 per year to partners in the South. At the high end were two independents: Central Jersey, which in 1991 sent $20,000 in cash and $100,000 in in-kind assistance to Masaya, Nicaragua; and New Haven, which gave Leon aid worth $250,000.

8. *The independents are more likely than the SCI affiliates to view development as a political process.* Two-thirds of the independents deem "working on joint political projects, such as monitoring human rights abuses or ending a war" a "very important" objective for development, while two-thirds of the SCI affiliates consider such projects "unimportant." When asked about their criteria for specific projects, well over half the independents expressed interest in promoting human rights, democracy, and peaceful conflict resolution, while less than a quarter of the SCI affiliates did.

9. *Few respondents see development as a two-way process.* Are US partners open to being developed *by* the South? Two out of three respondents showed some

sensitivity to this issue by saying that one of their objectives is to "solve mutual economic problems." But only eight of the 67 respondents said that they "design projects that enable those living in your partner city to support economic development in your own community." Six were SCI affiliates that were referring to projects that result in mutually beneficial *business* development. But what is good for business is not always what is good for people-centered development. Louisville, for example, insists on using its own consultants, materials, and supplies for projects in Quito, Ecuador – a practice that hinders people-centered development by reducing the self-reliance of its partners.

Only two respondents, both independents, indicated that they were using sister-city programs to support a vision of mutual economic development broader than business development, and both were located in Seattle. The committee overseeing Seattle's partnership with Daliwe in South Africa works closely with the Black Dollar Days Task Force, a group promoting economic empowerment of African Americans living in Seattle. The Seattle–Managua sister-city program tries to link minority and women's businesses in Seattle with grassroots enterprises in Managua.

One positive aspect of this survey was that it was one of the first times that SCI and the independents had collaborated closely. The survey revealed that the two networks each have distinct strong points. The SCI affiliates have succeeded in recruiting volunteers, involving the business community, providing technical assistance, and evaluating projects jointly. The independents have succeeded in raising funds, educating the public, lobbying national officials, avoiding red tape, and planning projects jointly. Participants in both networks are beginning to recognize that the two sides can benefit if knowledge is pooled, mistakes shared, and greater cooperation undertaken.

Zambia

Several features of Zambia's recent past have opened up the country to international ties. As a former British colony, Zambia has myriad connections with the United Kingdom and with other Anglophone countries. It shares some of the culture, laws, and administrative practices of Commonwealth countries. Its proximity to "hot spots" in southern Africa has made it an important ally for opponents of white supremacy in former Rhodesia and South Africa and for supporters of liberation movements in neighboring Angola, Mozambique, Zimbabwe, and Namibia. Western indifference or hostility to these movements motivated Zambia to set up ties with the Soviet Union, Eastern Europe, China, and Cuba. More recently Zambia has strengthened its linkages with other developing nations, particularly those in Africa, through bodies such as the

Non-Aligned Movement, the Organization for African Unity, the Southern Africa Development Coordinating Conference, and the Preferential Trade Area.

Many international actors are now working in Zambia. The World Bank and the International Monetary Fund are overseeing projects, loans, and structural-adjustment programs in the country. Ten major volunteer agencies from the North have projects in Zambia, including the British Voluntary Service Oversees (VSO), the Canadian University Service Overseas, and the Danish Volunteers Service. These agencies, along with many other NGOs and professional groups – Cuban doctors, French teachers, Mennonite missionaries, Finnish water engineers – have created a diverse landscape for North–South cooperation. Inevitably these organizations and individuals collaborate with Zambian NGOs and local governments. Some Zambian town councils have even retained foreign professionals to address specific development problems. The British VSO, for example, has been providing engineering advice to a consortium of provincial councils called the Integrated Rural Development Programme.

Linkages between foreign NGOs and Zambian communities have not been restricted to economic development. Theater groups from Scandinavia and Southern Africa have met in Lusaka, thanks to the organizing work of the Frontline Theater of Finland. The Zambian–India Friendship Associate (ZIFA) hosts Indians visiting Zambia, maintains a network of Zambians who have visited India, and assists Indians trying to settle in Zambia. Through the efforts of ZIFA, Indians have built a primary school in Lusaka, donated medical equipment to the Lusaka University Teaching Hospital, given scholarships for Zambians to study in India, and helped Zambians participate in the Olympic Games.

Recent political developments in Zambia have influenced the direction of its linking and twinning programs. In 1980 local governments were "unified" with the national government and the ruling party, and consequently districts became more important local political units than cities. Greater centralization could have meant that the district governors would use their new powers to ensure that rural areas and small towns (which had previously been of little interest to foreign communities) were equally represented in linking and twinning programs. But this never happened. Zambia's twinnings have involved only the largest, most accessible cities in the country.

Today, the largest urban areas in Zambia have multiple international partners while rural areas have none. Lusaka has twelve international twinning relationships, Ndola eight, Livingstone four, and Kitwe six. Among the most popular twinning partners are communities in Kenya, Liberia, Malawi, Portugal, Romania, the Soviet Union, the United Kingdom, United States, Yugoslavia, and Zaire.

Many of these twinnings grew out of Zambia's other long-standing international relationships. Lusaka's ties with Georgetown in Guyana evolved from relations between the Guyanan youth movement and the country's youth organization, the Zambian National Service. Zambia's links with Yugoslavia began with the creation of ZECCO, an engineering and construction firm jointly owned and operated by the two countries. Twinnings with Zaire were rooted in close linguistic and cultural ties between tribes in the two nations. Links with Malawi were based on the historical fact that many Malawians had worked in Zambia's mines and industries in the 1950s (the main African languages in the two countries are also similar).

Twinning ties have usually meant town officials visiting one another, but other CDI activities have occurred as well. Los Angeles provided Lusaka with books for its city library, medicines and artificial limbs for its hospitals, and a water engineer to help design a flood-control plan. Kamploops in Canada trained municipal engineers and financial officers from Lusaka.

Lusaka's ties with Lilongwe in Malawi suggest future possibilities for South–South cooperation. Councilors in the two cities have visited one another, and young Lusakan musicians and actors have performed in Lilongwe. The water departments in the two cities also have worked together.

Lusaka's relationship with Dushanbe, formerly in the Soviet Union and now part of Tadzhikistan, is a good example of East–South cooperation. In honor of its friends from Central Asia, Lusaka named one of its streets Dushanbe Road. In 1990 five members of the Lusaka city staff studied motor mechanics, carpentry, pharmaceuticals, and tanning in Dushanbe, and now Dushanbe expects to send several of its municipal staff for on-the-job training in the Lusaka city government. As noted earlier, Dushanbe sent $200,000-worth of emergency aid when floods hit Lusaka in 1989, and Lusaka returned the favor by sending consignments of fruits and vegetables when food shortages occurred in Dushanbe in December 1990. Lusaka now plans to pay for several Tadzhikistani students to attend the University of Zambia.

Zambians are ambivalent about what directions linking should take in the future. On the one hand, the severe poverty in the country makes linking with richer communities in the North – and the promise of aid and technical assistance – very attractive. On the other hand, closer ties with communities in the South and the East could be more balanced and rewarding in non-financial ways. Zambians also recognize the need for existing twinning programs to involve a wider range of participants, such as young people, the disabled, and women, and for new programs to connect rural areas and small towns.

Zimbabwe

Despite substantial economic progress since achieving independence in 1980, most Zimbabweans continue to live in poverty and the income distribution in the country is one of the most unequal in Africa. Zimbabwe is a country of 10 million people, three-quarters of whom live in rural areas.

The ongoing migration of workers from rural to urban areas has necessitated that development in both the cities and the countryside be overseen by the same governmental body: the Ministry of Local Government, Rural, and Urban Development. Working alongside NGOs, the Ministry has helped villages in Zimbabwe gain access to clean water, hygienic toilets, and good health centers. Zimbabwe's recent commitments to the international banking community to undertake "structural adjustment," however, have required cutbacks in social services that have slowed development.

Northern NGOs such as Oxfam-UK and Hivos have played an important role in Zimbabwe's development by providing funds for projects, some of which involve neighboring countries. Using finance from the Netherlands Organization for International Development Cooperation (NOVIB), for example, a number of NGOs formed the Southern Africa Nongovernmental Development Organizations in Relation with Novib (SANDON).

Even though Zimbabwe local authorities often do not officially acknowledge their collaboration with NGOs, they realize that NGOs are needed to solve many of the country's most pressing problems, such as unemployment, squatters, street children, and pollution. Local authorities have helped community groups by authorizing street collections and parades, by sharing information, by giving professional guidance, and by opening up municipal land and buildings for NGO use. In some cases international NGOs have financed joint action. The International Voluntary Services (IVS), for example, supported joint action to set up community cooperatives, and the Swedish Library Association helped Zimbabwean local authorities and women's clubs to set up adult literacy programs.

One place where local authorities can discuss possibilities for joint action is at the meetings of the District Development Committees. Each committee includes representatives of the national development ministries, local governments, NGOs, and church groups.

The National Association of Nongovernmental Organizations helps NGOs maintain a high profile within Zimbabwe. And a number of regional networks, such as the African Association for Literacy and Adult Education, Development Innovations and Networks in East and Southern Africa (IRED), and the All Africa Conference of Churches link Zimbabwean NGOs with NGOs of neighboring countries.

NGOs in Zimbabwe have had a profound impact on local, national, and international policy. Through extensive lobbying, the National Council for Disabled Persons of Zimbabwe has helped bring to the disabled, particularly those in rural areas, equal opportunities to work, to compete in sports, to attend school, and to use public transportation. The Women's Action Group shares its newsletter, *Speak Out*, with women's groups in Tanzania and Uganda.

Each of the nine largest cities in Zimbabwe has at least one twinning relationship abroad. Harare has six, Mutare has four, and Bulawayo and Gweru both have two. Most of Zimbabwe's twinnings are with English-speaking countries

(Canada, the Netherlands, the United Kingdom, and the United States), and all but one were initiated from the outside.

Generally, twinning relationships have led to visits by mayors and city officials, exchanges of municipal staff, and cultural programs. In some instances communities abroad have provided aid. Harare, for example, has received a fire-engine from Nottingham, a telex machine from Columbus, and a fax machine from Cincinnati. Basildon gave Gweru an Information Technology Centre with 19 computers. Aberdeen sent Bulawayo a fire-engine, equipment for the handicapped, library books, and clothing, and is now recruiting its retired technical staff to work in Bulawayo.

Gladys Maseko, Administrative Secretary for Africa Community-Based Development Initiatives writes:

> Aid has been found to be unavoidable in twinning relationships as long as the position of the South remains that of less privileged, less vocal, less organized, and less powerful, all because of the lack of resources. One Northern partner said that his community sees aid as "hand ups" to propel the South to self-reliance, as opposed to "hand outs" which are piecemeal.

Donations often come *from* Zimbabwe as well. A school in Mutare sent traditional musical instruments to its twinning partners in Tameside. Other Zimbabwean gifts have included arts, crafts, and hides. As Maseko notes, however: "Generally the Zimbabwean local authorities were not aware of the value of their contribution to their Northern links, including the information (a very powerful force) and the legitimacy that they [provided] to the Northern initiatives."

Women in Zimbabwe have been key players in the development of the country. Because so many men work in the cities, rural development in particular is the responsibility of women. NGOs such as Women's Action Groups have lobbied the government to ensure equal rights for women. The Young Women's Christian Association has lobbied the South African government, among others, to release political prisoners.

Zimbabweans generally seem satisfied with their CDIs but have voiced criticisms in three areas. First, some Zimbabwe partners feel frustrated about the degree of control Northerners exercise over CDIs. According to one writer, "NGO funds are not in the hands of local people. The lion's share is in foreign hands and local NGOs have very little resources."

Second, many Zimbabweans are uncomfortable with the large role of aid in twinning relationships. Maseko writes: "Twinning arrangements where nothing had been donated were described as inactive. Preoccupation with material gains tends to overshadow other areas of possible mutual benefits." It also causes Zimbabweans to undervalue the possible benefits from South–South linking. One local authority apparently turned down a link with a Southern town because "there is nothing to benefit from that link." A twinning relationship should move beyond projects and aid, Maseko argues, "to a more fundamental exchange on the causes of poverty and the nature of its alleviation."

Finally, community groups in Zimbabwe are eager for greater grassroots participation. Most twinning arrangements involve mayors and council members, but not community groups.

Joint action has become easier since the Conference on South–North International Linking for Development was held in Bulawayo in November 1990. That gathering was a watershed event in Zimbabwe and led to the formation of a new NGO to coordinate CDIs in southern Africa called African Community-based Development Initiatives (ACDI): A Network of Action for a New World Order. Thus far, ACDI has helped communities and African NGOs share information and collaborate, and it has motivated more local authorities to "take the link to the people."

CDI Declarations

The Cologne Appeal: From Charity to Justice

The representatives of NGOs and local authorities from nine European countries adopted this appeal at the First European Conference on Towns and Development in Cologne, Germany, on September 19, 1985. This appeal is addressed to local authorities, non-governmental organizations, and community groups throughout Europe.

Preamble

In view of the existing situation between North and South in which there is:

- growing disparity in basic human needs;
- the non-existence of a meaningful North–South dialogue;
- the inability of existing structures to cope with the magnitude and urgency of a grave situation which results in hunger, starvation, famine, population problems, and environmental destruction, all being the consequence of poverty related to the existing world economic order;
- the escalating problem of the loss of dignity, and even of life, for millions of people.

For moral reasons and international solidarity, as well as the mutual interest of removing threats to peace, a higher political priority must be given to the search for urgent and sustainable solutions to these problems. The Conference is fully aware that, without structural change in many fields of policy related to the North–South problem, the intolerable situation will escalate. It also recognizes that, while aid is welcome and necessary for those who suffer from injustice, aid is insufficient for achieving a genuine solution. All too often aid can be used as an alibi to ease the conscience of the North. Nevertheless, the quantity and quality of aid must be improved. In any event, money by itself is not enough. Change requires the active participation of people in both South and North, learning from each other.

The Conference further recognizes that the interrelations of the problems of environment, development, and disarmament must also be taken into account in any analysis of the North–South relationship.

Therefore, the Conference welcomes the recommendations of the Florence Conference on Towns and Cooperation for Development of October 1983 appealing to and encouraging local authorities to stimulate and support local North–South activities together with non-government organizations (NGOs). This process of decentralization is seen as the starting-point and challenge for raising public awareness leading to a more comprehensive understanding of North–South problems (including the problems in the North), extending beyond the concept of aid, and mobilizing people in direct action for change and partnership.

This new approach of decentralizing the North–South cooperation, which focuses on cooperation between NGOs and towns, includes an important role for the rural communities, North and South, in the processes of development and social change. NGOs are fully aware that this is a supplement to and not a substitute for governmental action at the national and international level.

In the light of these considerations this Conference calls upon development groups and local authorities to initiate and sustain NGO and local community joint action for North–South cooperation based on justice instead of charity.

Objectives

Such joint action may take a variety of forms including information, education, linking, campaigning and project activities.

Information activities embrace materials, events, courses, etc. designed to increase public awareness of North–South issues. Specifically, support should be given to the establishment of local and regional information, documentation, and service centers to enable individuals and groups to learn more about the developing world.

Education activities include both formal and informal learning which creates a critical understanding to spur direct action for change. Development education in the North is essential for decision-making with a global perspective.

Linking activities can involve all sectors of local communities in establishing friendship, solidarity, and partnership with towns and rural areas in the South on a community-to-community basis. Such increased mutual understanding leads to cooperative ventures, including intermunicipal cooperation based on an informed and realistic appreciation of each other's society.

Campaigning activities call for policy changes to secure greater equity in international relationships in areas such as the right of developing countries to build up their society. Campaigns also need to recognize the need for structural change in the international economic and social order with implications for our own societies.

Project activities should be subject to clearly defined criteria and involve the full participation of NGOs and local communities, both North and South. Local authorities in the North wishing to support development projects or linking are encouraged to consult and involve experienced NGOs and local linking committees.

Process

Survey. Municipal governments, together with NGOs, are advised to survey the existing North–South links – political, economic, social, cultural, and educational – in their communities and assess the need to and possibilities for expanding these links.

Policy Plan. NGO–local authority action in this field can be based on a policy plan jointly formulated and officially adopted by the town council in order to stimulate public discussion. Initial cooperative actions may precede the establishment of such policy plans.

Linking. Effective linking implies the full participation of all sectors of both communities such as schools, workers' organizations, political parties, women's groups, youth, church, professional and employer organizations, and the media. In effective city-to-city twinning the NGOs and the local community must also be involved.

Minorities. Joint action in this field should also recognize and address the problems and contributions of foreign minorities living in our societies. The need for development education and action is related to the need to combat discrimination, racism and poverty in industrialized countries.

Funding. While the principal aim of this type of cooperation is not primarily the demand for finance of NGO activities by local authorities, minimum budgets need to be debated and established for both development information/education and for implementation of sustainable development projects. Given the trend towards the increased commercialization of aid and the tendency to freeze or reduce development assistance, especially to the poorest countries, there is a danger that NGO projects are arrested before reaching fruition. Further study is needed to determine what are the most effective forms of local, regional, national and European co-financing plans.

Project Guidelines. Many Northern-based NGOs, together with their partners in the South, have elaborated important criteria for supporting development projects based on such broad principles as the following:

- equality, reciprocity, absence of paternalism;
- initiation and approval of projects by the partner communities;
- focus on the poorest in the developing countries and the poorest countries;
- recognition of the significance of women in the development process and ensurance that projects benefit and enhance the status of women;
- the need to take account of the environmental impact of projects in advance;

- integration of projects into the overall development plans of the partner community;
- establishing and maintaining communications;
- the need to respect and maintain cultural diversity;
- the need for joint evaluation.

The Partnership

Joint action between NGOs and local authorities in this field requires a genuine partnership to assure a competent and accountable use of resources.

It is recommended that NGOs join and establish platforms and networks, especially at the local level. NGOs should allocate resources to coordinate their activities and put forward joint views more effectively. Similarly, local authorities should also raise and promote these issues in their regional and national associations.

Local NGO platforms are to be as broad as possible with groups concerned with peace, economic, and environmental questions invited to join. The platform can stimulate discussions with local councils and regional assemblies.

Where possible, local authorities should appoint persons responsible for North–South relations and persons to liaise with NGOs and implement joint actions.

Follow-up

This appeal is addressed to local authorities, NGOs and community groups throughout Europe. It is intended to invigorate the process of promoting NGO–local community joint action. The results of the Conference can serve as a basis for NGO approaches to local authorities to call for active campaigns and initiatives such as community-to-community linking for North–South cooperation.

The Conference asks the organizing committee to stand ready to assist NGOs and local authorities wishing to follow up the Conference at the regional and national levels, but the initiative for such follow-up must come from the local level. In particular, local NGOs should approach their communities with proposals for joint action.

The European Community and the Council of Europe should be encouraged to lend their support to these efforts.

The Conference participants stress that in undertaking this type of North–South cooperation it is of vital importance to discuss fully the implications with their counterparts in the South at all stages.

In all of the foregoing the Conference is acutely aware that in the end it is people working together who will demand and bring about change for sustainable development and a just and equitable society. Thus, any machinery developed to implement the resolutions above will fail unless it is based on the potential and participation of the individual.

The Bulawayo Appeal: From Dependency to Justice

The South–North International Conference on Linking for Development held in Bulawayo from 28th to 30th November 1990 was attended by 100 participants from local authorities and NGOs from 25 countries: twelve African states, Lebanon, nine European countries, USA, and the Caribbean. The Conference was organized by Zimbabwe-based representatives of local authorities and NGOs and was hosted by the Organization of Rural Associations for Progress (ORAP), with the support of the Commonwealth Secretariat, Towns and Development, Oxfam, Christian Aid and Bulawayo City Council. The conference agreed unanimously on the following Appeal.

Preamble

The Conference notes with concern:

- The global trend toward further widening of the gap between South and North which is a result of the existing world economic disorder, especially the debt crisis, which also has far-reaching consequences.
- The rapid changes in the relationship between East and West with all the resultant opportunities and threats.
- The ongoing Northern tendency toward the destruction of resources, and consumer patterns, a tendency which the East is now in danger of following and a tendency which is growing stronger than ever in the South.
- The fact that warnings about ecological damage are constantly ignored and will remain unheeded until the North changes its attitude and accepts the principle of equitable and sustainable sharing of the world's resources.
- The threatening destruction of the environment as a result of exploitation and underdevelopment.
- The unresponsiveness of the North to the growing demand for the South to take full control of its destiny and to cooperate with Southern partners directly.
- The refusal to accept the right of the people in the South to regain human dignity and freedom from all forms of exploitation.
- That international conferences including UN forums have been largely unsuccessful in achieving concrete solutions.

The participation of people at a local level in any program aimed at global development and change is required more than ever before, in order that more pressure is exerted on national and international institutions and governments.

Linking for Development is an appropriate tool to organize people's participation both in the South and in the North.

Principles

- While South–North links for development are desirable, they must be founded on clear principles of mutual respect, honesty, trust, reciprocity, and fairness between the parties involved.
- Linking for development is a marriage of interests. The parties involved should therefore participate on equal terms and ensure that two-way communication is paramount.
- There is a need to instill self-pride and dignity in the people living in the South and to redress the adverse psychological effects of relationships both in the South and in the North.
- Both the South and the North have a responsibility and accountability toward their respective constituents and to each other.
- In order to attain sustainable development there is a need for the South to strive toward material independence through greater reliance on local resources and through South–South cooperation.
- South–North relationships should be based on the right of people to decide for themselves about their own destiny. Development should therefore be seen as a response to the needs of people as a whole.
- South–North linking for development should focus primarily on human relationships and dignity as basic to any material exchange, technological transfer, and technical assistance programs.
- There is a need for surveys, analysis, and debate in both the South and the North before concrete linking arrangements are concluded. The partners involved must have a clear vision and clear objectives.
- Partners at both ends of South–North Linking for Development share a common commitment to support each other with a view to achieving their common goals.
- South–North Linking for Development partnerships should take account of the dynamic nature of human needs and must stand open to adjustment and reorientation when new ones arise.

Issues

All participants commit themselves to the implementation of the following agenda:

Human Rights and Dignity. Commitment to the campaign against apartheid, its institutions, and all other forms of racism and oppression, and to the support of all efforts to establish a world in which human rights and dignity are respected and promoted.

The Environment. Grassroots awareness should be raised on environmental issues which affect both South and North through lobbying for sustainable environmental protection. This requires: a change of attitudes, practices and consumer patterns in the North; actions to encourage the lobbying of corporations, multinationals, utilities, and national governments to adopt clear and sustainable policies and practices; encouraging teachers to use suitable material in schools to ensure that children develop this awareness at their earliest possible stages; videos highlighting environmental issues; and positive environmentally friendly campaign posters, calendars, postcards, pamphlets, etc.

Development. Initiation and support of all efforts to empower people to enhance their quality of life both in the South and North in response to their cultural and socioeconomic needs. Acceptance and promotion of the important role of women in development. Women should be involved in the planning and implementation processes.

Education and Training. The provision of development education for people in local communities and institutions both in the North and in the South highlighting: images and stereotypes (negative and positive); health issues; intercultural issues; and apartheid and all other racist and oppressive systems. The provision of knowledge and skills to those members of the communities and institutions who are most educationally disadvantaged. The provision of education and the raising of awareness about issues concerning the present world order such as: unfair trade between North and South; debt problems that perpetuate the dependency of the South on the North; and the exploitative nature of the global operation of multinational corporations.

Strategies

- The starting point for local South–South and South–North activities varies from community to community depending on existing structures, motivations, and dedication of individuals in local authorities and NGOs.
- Wherever possible, both sides should cooperate as closely as possible in order to reach all levels of society in towns, regions and communities.
- Development cooperation at the local level tries to link NGOs and local authorities, individuals, institutions, media, unions, appropriate commercial sectors, and communities. People's participation on ground of common interests stabilizes democratic structures and allows constant information flow and exchange for global action at the local level.

- South–North information exchange will certainly enrich the societies in the South and North and can help them better to understand global interdependence and responsibility.
- Experience has shown that clearly defined aims and objectives on both sides help to avoid misunderstandings, overexpectations, and frustrations.
- Regular evaluation at each end of the link is the appropriate tool for learning, understanding, improving, and strengthening the partnerships at all levels.
- Setting up of networks with other communities and institutions which deal with similar issues and concerns. Northern partners should be ready to support institution building at local, regional, and intercontinental levels.
- Local and regional authorities in the South and North should take on the responsibility of lobbying governments and parliaments for change of global policies.

The existing world order is structured and controlled to benefit the North; it will be impossible to change this injustice without constant popular pressure at a grassroots level.

Priorities and Implementation Strategies

The Conference resolves to establish an International African Committee for South–South and North–South Linking for Development networking and action.

The Conference:

- recognizes the need for a focal point at the national level and urges that national committees be established in Africa to fulfil that role;
- requests the Committee to identify existing linking and networking organizations in the South and in the North;
- requests the Committee to explore how best to achieve a viable and sustainable support structure for Linking for Development in Africa;
- requests the Committee to consult with the OAU, Preferential Trade Areas (PTA), ECOWAS, SADCC, and other African structures such as the Maghreb Union to support South–South and South–North development initiatives;
- requests the Committee in the light of the outcome of these consultations, to draw up proposals for detailed implementation of the strategies identified in this Appeal;
- urges the Secretary General of the United Nations and the Director of the United Nations Environment Programme (UNEP) to ensure that concerns expressed in the "Bulawayo Appeal" are incorporated into the activities of the International Council for Local Environmental Initiatives;

- urges the initiators of this Conference to encourage and support similar regional Linking for Development conferences in other parts of Africa, Asia, and Latin America;
- urges the initiators of this Conference to encourage and foster any other issues/action that will encourage and promote South–South and South–North Links for Development.

The Sevagram Declaration: Ideals to Action

The following appeal was adopted at a National Workshop on Sustainable Development, which took place in Sevagram, India, on March 14-17, 1992.

Preamble

Recognizing the significance of this Conference assembling in Sevagram, the village settlement founded by Mahatma Gandhi, who stood for the eternal values of truth and non-violence and the active principles of love and service for the establishment of a *New World Order*:

- realizing the need for progress and development to be based on respect for the human personality, the dignity of labor, and democratic norms for the functioning of a free society;
- conscious of the necessity to maintain ecological balance, preserve and promote purity of environment, and conserve energy and resources;
- bearing in mind the importance of the family as the basic unit of society and the foundation for cooperative and cohesive community life;
- aware of the imperative need to avoid exploitation of any kind of man by man and group by group;
- concerned with the growing hiatus between the countries in the North and the South in terms of quality of life, perceptions of development, prerequisites for progress and parameters of wants and necessities;
- anxious to halt further impoverishment of the people, especially in the South, through adoption of measures which can only increase the crisis of fiscal deficit, balance of payments, debt trap, inflation, and growing unemployment and the consequent destruction of even the subsistence and survival economy prevalent today;
- mindful of the fact that undernourishment, malnutrition, ill health, and illiteracy have to be eradicated if the society in the South is to regain its lost vitality, autonomy, and identity and march forward with firm steps and with its head held high;
- aware of the distortions in the discourses on development presented to dominant interests, external and internal;

- rejecting Consumerism and Commercialism as the inevitable concomitants to the process of development;
- becoming wiser by learning from the failure of the ill-conceived models of development in the North and the newly industrialized countries and the consequent alienation of people from people within countries and among nations;
- accepting the desirability of maximum devolution of political power and decentralization of economic activities through plurality of institutions, traditional but imbued with a commonality of purpose so that small communities can come into their own and not get marginalized in the name of Globalization;
- noticing the enormous possibility for cooperation between people through local initiatives in the North and the South, particularly from the point of view of self-sufficiency and self-reliance in a spirit of equality and partnership and through the development of appropriate structures and institutions, tactics, and strategies;
- valuing the enormous contribution that can be made for sustainable development through small towns, Panchayats, tribal councils, and villages as autonomous units, and understanding the need for establishing the necessary channels for articulating the aspirations of the disadvantaged sections of society.

This conference of 100 representatives of voluntary organizations, official agencies, and local bodies declares its firm resolve to strive in all possible ways to promote South–South and South–North cooperation and mutual assistance for furthering the cause of sustainable development and appeals to the United Nations to take all essential steps to preserve peace, maintain harmony, and accelerate international understanding and cooperation on the basis of the objectives contained in this declaration.

Action Plan

By and large it was suggested by the delegates to plan and achieve the following:
At NGOs Level. (1) Promotion of solidarity through exchange visits, placement of volunteers, officials, and others from voluntary agencies. (2) To plan appropriate actions for Environment Campaign. (3) To study and plan actions for promotion of effective North and South Dialogue and promote more exchange and visits. (4) The exchange and dialogue could be with small, medium, and large NGOs and other international Agencies. (5) Promote more contacts with government and local authorities.
At Local Authority Level. (1) More exchange of ideas on various issues and planning actions for restoring the power authorities of local officials. (2) Should establish contacts with local NGOs and government authorities and promote effective collaboration between them. (3) Should have specific projects on environment and human rights.

At Government Level. (1) The government must recognize that unless the local authorities and NGOs are taken into confidence, no development will be possible anywhere and, therefore, the government must plan its activities and plans in consultation with the NGOs and local authorities. (2) All governments must have good contact with national-level NGOs and local-level organizations so that they are aware of their roles in development.

Strategy of Work. It is suggested that an office of Towns and Development be established in India with a view to promoting the concept through it. Once the office is established, it is observed that a number of units could be established in the region and appropriate plans made and established. The office to be established in India will be able to establish contacts with other NGOs, local authorities, and governments for future activities in the area of sustainable development.

Main Issues and Activities. (1) Training of volunteers/officials on various issues connected with sustainable development. (2) Preparation of Media Pack for public consumption. (3) Promotion of village-level organizations. (4) Developing traditional skills and approaches for sustainable development. (5) Promotion of Sanitation Program. (6) Undertaking linking program for effective consolidation and collaboration between NGOs. (7) Undertaking activities for environmental campaign, human development, social justice.

The Berlin Charter: Joint Action for Sustainable Development

Preamble

We, the delegates and participants from 53 countries in North, South, West and East, gathered in Berlin in the International North–South Conference "Local Initiatives for Sustainable Development" on 14-17 October 1992, declare our commitment to undertake joint action for sustainable development. In making this declaration, we invite others not represented at this conference to join us in following the principles and the action agenda set out below.

The Challenge

Dynamic processes, such as the changes in Central and Eastern Europe, the intensification of the fight against apartheid, racism, and oppression and the removal of juntas and corrupt dictatorships, testify to hard work on the long and difficult process of establishing and anchoring democracy. At the same time, in many parts of Africa, Asia, and Latin America barriers to change are coming down. All involved in these changes deserve our full support.

The transition symbolized by the fall of the Berlin Wall also opened the way for the other necessary change at the global level – the demolition of the economic wall dividing humanity between North and South. Yet on the 500th anniversary of Columbus's voyage and in the city which in 1884 saw the arbitrary colonial division of the African continent at the Berlin Congo Conference, we recognize that the "New International Economic Order" is far from being achieved. Some 20 percent of the world's population consume most of the resources, while 80 percent live in or near poverty.

The majority in the North and the elite in the South take a privileged lifestyle for granted. In the South the majority still have to struggle for survival. This situation is a form of global social and economic apartheid which leaves millions destitute, unemployed, homeless, and malnourished.

Today, according to the 1992 Human Development Report of the United Nations Development Program, the nations of the South face a crushing burden of US$ 1.5 trillion of debt, and official aid has done little to reverse the flow of resources from South to North. In 1990 alone, the South transferred an estimated US$ 250 billion to the North and only received official development aid of US$ 54 billion. Even this low level of aid is now under threat and will drop below half of 0.7 percent of GNP if no corrective action is taken. To produce the trade surpluses necessary to service these debts, the International Monetary Fund and World Bank have forced the South to accept harsh structural adjustment measures that further increase suffering and poverty.

The application of structural adjustment policies has severely aggravated the effects of poverty which, together with the problems of debt and unfair trade, has contributed further to the degradation of the human condition and the environment. Moreover, as the Brundtland Commission warned, continuation of "business as usual" will further deplete the ozone layer, dangerously alter the planet's climate, and jeopardize the survival of many species. These issues were addressed at the United Nations Conference on Environment and Development (UNCED, the Rio Earth Summit, 1992) which adopted Agenda 21 saying, *inter alia*:

> Because so many of the problems and solutions being addressed by Agenda 21 have their roots in local activities, the participation and cooperation of local authorities will be a determining factor in fulfilling its objectives. Local authorities construct, operate and maintain economic, social and environmental policies and regulations, and assist in implementing national and sub-national environmental policies. As the level of government closest to the people, they play a vital role in educating, mobilizing and responding to the public to promote sustainable development.
>
> By 1996, most local authorities in each country should have undertaken a consultative process with their populations and achieved a consensus on a "local Agenda 21" for the community.

At present, development is promoted by many through so-called free markets but these may in practice handicap fair trade. The General Agreement on Tariffs and Trade, for example, allows companies to operate freely across borders with too little regard to workers, consumers, or the environment. Communities in both North and South engage in destructive competition to attract corporations by accepting poor working conditions and low environmental standards. The European Single Market also has disadvantageous implications for the South.

There is little time left to change course. Although the Cold War has ended, global military expenditure remains at the level of US$ 1.3 trillion, while global development programs are starved of funds. Widespread movement towards democracy, despite many shortcomings, opens up new possibilities for action which will help guarantee human rights and promote sustainable development. This movement has not yet been matched in the international institutions, notably the United Nations Security Council. Local democracy and citizens' participation are key components of any democratic system. NGOs, community groups, and local authorities, being closest to the people, are in a unique position to enhance public understanding of the world's problems and to facilitate individual and collective local action for change.

The potential for worldwide action may be judged by the response to our earlier appeals articulated at Cologne, Bulawayo, and Sevagram. Many communities have expressed their support for those appeals and have begun to participate in practical action on North–South issues, working through new partnership structures.

Rationale for Action

Why should community groups, local authorities, and NGOs act to end the present destructive course?

- because all humanity shares responsibility in the quest for planetary survival;
- because the daily quest for survival consumes all the energies of large numbers of people in the South;
- because the planet's resources are finite and cannot sustain lifestyles characterized by overconsumption and waste, primarily in the North;
- because the major environmental problems of global warming, ozone depletion, acid rain, and threats to biodiversity affect all in our local communities;
- because continuation of the present course will further accelerate environmental degradation, increase tensions between nations and regions, and ruin the lives of millions;
- because the short-term policies of public authorities at all levels have failed so far to address North–South issues adequately;
- because to stand by and watch from a comfortable position while others suffer and struggle is unacceptable;

- because conflicts, wars, environmental degradation, and political and economic oppression often lead to large-scale displacement of people, including minorities and indigenous peoples;
- because our schools, our universities, our businesses, our local authorities and other local institutions are integral parts of the international community;
- because all communities have specific know-how and skills that can be shared with others elsewhere in the world;
- because citizenship in a democracy carries the obligation for each individual to act responsibly.

Guiding Principles

We call on communities North and South, West and East, to review and remake relations between the rich and poor of the world based on the following principles:

Democracy. Policies can only be responsive to people's needs if every citizen can participate in the formulation and implementation of policies through decentralized structures and with free access to information, and if democracy and human rights are respected.

Sustainability. All life depends on the health of the earth's ecosystems, which are now being severely damaged. Lifestyles, spending patterns, production methods, and the use of natural resources should no longer be allowed to jeopardize the welfare of present and future generations.

Justice. Until just political, economic, and social institutions are achieved to counter inequalities, sustainable development cannot be assured.

Fairness. Global resources must be fairly shared, so that all people – regardless of gender, age, disability, class, caste, religion, race, or ethnic origin – can lead a decent life.

Tolerance. Communities in the East, West, South, and North should join forces in combatting racism, xenophobia, and other forms of intolerance and social exclusion.

Joint Action. Community groups, local authorities, and NGOs each have special skills and expertise which, when brought together on the basis of mutual respect, reciprocity, and grassroots participation, can facilitate powerful collective action.

Interdependence. Communities in the North, South, East, and West should join forces in the spirit of interdependence and self-reliance, with due respect for democratic and cultural values and the rights of minorities.

Framework for Action

Towns and Development, with representatives duly nominated by all the regions, has drawn up a comprehensive Action Agenda based on the recommendations made by the 42 working groups meeting during the Conference. The Action Agenda sets out a range of possible steps to be taken by community groups, local authorities and non-governmental organizations under the following broad headings:

Sustainable Behavior. Communities should become globally responsible by requiring public and private sector organizations in their areas to minimize pollution of the biosphere and the consumption of non-renewable resources.

Awareness Raising. Communities should raise public awareness of North–South interdependence through maximum direct experience and discussion and by educational activities both inside and outside educational institutions at all levels.

Twinning/Linking. Communities should increase understanding of other societies and cultures by twinning with partner communities and by fostering links between counterpart institutions of all kinds.

Technical Assistance. Communities should exchange staff with partner communities in a search for solutions to common problems.

Projects. Communities should support projects abroad, provided that they promote just and sustainable development and reflect the ongoing participation of the beneficiaries in planning, implementation, and evaluation.

Campaigning. Communities should build upon the North/South Campaign, One World 92, the UNCED-Agenda 21, and Local Agenda 21 processes, campaigns against apartheid and other human-rights campaigns, urging upon national, regional, and international leaders the need to lift debt burdens from the South and to strengthen international laws protecting workers, consumers, and the environment.

Networking. Communities should have effective access to international networks to share information and experience on specific international issues.

Fair Trading. Communities should take positive action to encourage good corporate environmental trading practice by their suppliers of goods and services, and should encourage citizens to do likewise.

Institution Building

Community action for just and sustainable development is strengthened by building strong, resilient political structures at the local level. The previous conferences in Cologne, Bulawayo, and Sevagram have underscored the need for local institutions to stimulate community initiative, to provide necessary resources, and to foster civil society. Democratically elected local authorities should be the expression of communities governing themselves, articulating the needs and aspirations of their areas, providing appropriate public services, and empowering local initiatives with their political influence, resources, and expertise. Informal institutions have an important complementary role.

Action in the following areas should be considered:

Local Forums. Setting up local coordinating structures comprising elected members and officers of local authorities and representatives of NGOs, private sector organizations, trade unions, and community groups who can help conceive, implement, and evaluate the community's North–South activities.

Allocation of Responsibility. Designating an appropriate person within the local authority to be responsible for environment and development.

Public Hearings. Holding public hearings on the impact of global issues on the local community which will help in the formulation of local plans for sustainable development.

Regular Monitoring. Producing an annual "state of the city in the world" report that can be distributed to citizens throughout the community.

Regional Structures. Forming regional structures on every continent to help communities to share experience and work together more effectively on North–South issues.

Universality

Following the series of previous conferences at Cologne, Bulawayo, and Sevagram, and bearing in mind the outcome of the East–West twinning conferences in Rotterdam and Prague, the time is ripe for a global approach. Thus, all these actions should be undertaken not only by the North but also by the South and the East. The growing number of communities involved in East–West twinning should consider implementing their programs in partnership with communities from the South. And wherever possible, the West and the East should support decentralized South–South action.

We, the delegates and participants in the conference, therefore:

- Call upon Towns and Development, working together with representatives from all regions and with the international groupings of local authorities and NGOs, to formulate strategies and programs during 1993 to implement this Berlin Charter and Action Agenda in the years ahead.
- Call upon local authorities, NGOs, and community groups to play their respective roles to the fullest in implementing this Charter and Action Agenda at the local, national, regional, and continental levels and to allocate adequate resources to this end.
- Urge that appropriate measures be taken to write off the international debts of the nations of the South.
- Urge all national governments in the North to fulfil the agreed UN target of 0.7 percent of GNP as official development assistance and to stop causing the South to suffer from the current economic problems in the North through cuts in such assistance.
- Urge that all unfair trade practices be removed.

- Urge all national governments and parliaments to pass legislation providing the legal and fiscal powers required, including where necessary a greater share of tax revenues, for local authorities, NGOs, and community groups to work together actively for sustainable development.
- Propose that the progress achieved in implementing the Berlin Charter and Action Agenda be systematically evaluated by all the partners at a further conference in due course.

The Berlin Action Agenda

Communities in North, South, East, and West should pursue action plans appropriate to their *local* circumstances, drawing upon the following recommended areas of activities:

Sustainable Behavior

- Encourage individuals to recognize their contribution to change as global citizens and to commit themselves to attain sustainable development.
- Establish a Local Agenda 21 (post UNCED) to call a halt to the further degradation of the human condition and the environment.
- Plan all projects and activities with consideration for any environmental impact.
- Initiate environmental activities within linking and twinning programs.
- Promote alternative energy sources.
- Introduce local bylaws to support sustainable development, e.g. on traffic, infrastructure, and housing.
- Initiate activities to alleviate poverty, provide shelter, and include basic human rights in programs for a sustainable environment.
- Identify, highlight, and develop traditional skills and approaches for sustainable development where possible.

Awareness Raising

- Promote and implement surveys of local South–North, North–South and North–South–East political, historical, social, cultural, and educational links and use this survey for awareness purposes (exhibitions, school projects, etc.).
- Promote educational programs which enable citizens to connect global issues to individual and local activities.
- Introduce North–South and North–South–East agendas with special attention for human rights and democracy, to training and education programs for council personnel/youth groups/women's groups/trade union groups etc, and set up courses and seminars for local teachers.
- Utilize existing charters/declarations, guidelines, and manuals to encourage active citizenship, human rights, and anti-racist educational programs.

- Set up resource centers for North–South and North–South–East issues and development education and strengthen existing ones.
- Allocate a percentage of your development education budgets in the North to facilitate development education in the South and East.
- Develop and disseminate effective strategies for use of (and advice in the use of) the mass media at the local and national levels.
- Encourage local media to introduce North–South and North–South–East issues into their education sections and programs.

Twinning/Linking

- Identify, analyze, and build on existing local links (North–South, South–South and South–East–West) where possible.
- Ground all twinnings and linkings in good human relationships that are characterized by careful planning, ongoing communication, and long-term commitment.
- Plan and implement all links with a step-by-step approach.
- Use both formal (local authority) and informal (NGO, community) approaches, but always ensure full participation of all sectors of both communities.
- Build broad, all-party support for links in order to ensure their continuity.
- Involve residents originating from other parts of the world and staying in the local area in your activities.
- Define in negotiation with partners precise aims and objectives and hold regular reviews of progress.
- Match similar organizations (schools, churches, voluntary organizations and trade unions, etc).
- Arrange visits as an integral part of linking but be careful not to restrict such exchanges to the official level and encourage the visiting party to stay with host families.
- Include awareness-raising events in partner visits.
- Recognize the crucial importance of South–South communication and provide support.
- Form joint delegations of local authorities and NGOs to monitor human rights/environment abuses (to protect local activists through the presence of outsiders).
- Consider taking up issues like the debt crisis, fair trade, and the effect of multinationals, etc in the framework of linking.
- Try where possible to create joint projects in which each partner can take parallel initiatives in its own community and investigate possibilities of including decentralized cooperation guidelines in mutual aid and projects.

Technical Assistance and Projects

- Research jointly the real needs of all partners involved, use clearly defined criteria, and consult experienced NGOs, local authorities, and other linking communities.
- Facilitate partners' participation in the planning and implementation of all programs.
- Design technical assistance programs with a maximum commitment to the empowerment of disadvantaged groups and the involvement of women.
- Fit programs into the wider local agenda and priorities of the partners.
- Recognize and use existing resources of all partners, jointly taking into account the dangers of creating dependency.
- Combine technical assistance and projects with development education programs.
- Provide information and guidelines to partners on decentralized cooperation programs and budget lines.
- Provide cross-cultural briefings for participants in technical cooperation schemes.
- De-brief participants in staff exchange programs and make use of their experience in awareness-raising programs.
- Encourage all partners involved to seek together solutions to problems both in the North and in the South.
- Liaise with local businesses to investigate possibilities for technical advice and assistance.

Campaigning

- Plan jointly, with local authority, community group, and NGO involvement, approaches to lobby for structural change in the economic and social order.
- Use coming UN "years" (e.g. Human Rights and Population) and the 50th anniversary of UN as foci for ongoing campaigns as well as current NGO campaigns.
- Include Southern participation in Northern campaigning activities where appropriate.
- Set up anti-discrimination projects.
- Support civic associations (e.g. in South Africa) in their claims for equal shares of municipal services and resources, maximum participation and control, accountable leadership, and education for empowerment.
- Promote compensation to the South for "environmentally friendly" economics.
- Campaign locally for widening of access to North–South, South–North and North–South–East awareness-raising information programs, events, and facilities.

Networking

- Local forums should include wider social groups (industry, commerce, women, youth, churches, trade unions) and formulate together with local authorities local plans for sustainable development.
- Ensure regular and effective dissemination of relevant information about local, national, and regional activities and about plans and concerns of partners.
- Seek structural and institutional support for Southern community-level action.
- International networks of local authorities, NGOs, and community groups should work together to facilitate the democratization processes directed at local level.
- Develop alternative forums to nurture the organic growth of alternatives to nationalism.

Fair Trading

- Encourage local authorities and NGOs to adopt "fair trade" purchasing policies and develop "fair trade" networks.
- Analyze/investigate North–South development policy and activities of local businesses.
- Contact local firms with export/import interests and use their contacts and know-how.
- Educate producers and consumers about need for Fair Trade.

Resources

Contacts in the North

AUSTRIA:
Brigid Weinzinger
Austrian Information Service on Development Policy (OIE)
Tuchlauben 8
1010 Vienna
Tel: +43/222-533375517
Fax: +43/222-533375521

Franz Schmidjell
Vienna Institute for Development Cooperation (VIDC)
Weyrgasse 5
1030 Vienna
Tel: +43/222-7133594
Fax: +43/222-7133573

BELGIUM:
Paul van Steenvoort
National Centre for Development Cooperation
De Vlasfabriekstraat 11
1060 Brussels
Tel: +32/2-5392620
Fax: +32/2-7391343

FINLAND:
Heikki Telakivi
Association of Finnish Municipalities
Toinen Linja 14
00530 Helsinki
Tel: +35/0-7712005
Fax: +35/0-7712053

Mikko Lohikoski
Finnish Volunteer Service (Kepa)
Frederikinkatu 63 A 8
00100 Helsinki
Tel: +358/0-6942745
Fax: +358/0-6941786

FRANCE:
Jean Louis Margerie
United Towns Organisation (UTO)
92300 Levallois Perret
Paris
Tel: +33/1-47393686
Fax: +33/1-42703799

GERMANY:
Gunther Hilliges
State Office of Development Cooperation Bremen
Slevogtstrasse 48
28209 Bremen
Tel: +49/421-3612194
Fax: +49/421-3612648

Climate Alliance
Philip Reisstrasse 84
60486 Frankfurt am Main
Tel: +49/692-1239461
Fax: +49/692-1239140

Jürgen Varnhorn
State Office of Development Cooperation Berlin
Martin Lutherstrasse 105
1000 Berlin
Tel: +49/30-7838270
Fax: +49/30-7838455

Gerold Weisrock
European Bureau for Municipal Development Cooperation of the City of
   Mainz
P.O. Box 3820
55028 Mainz
Tel: +49/6131-122375
Fax: +49/6131-122406

GREECE:
Pantelis Sklias
Hellenic Institute of Solidarity and Cooperation with Developing Countries
9 Orminioystreet
11528 Athens
Tel: +30/1-7234456
Fax: +30/1-7237662

IRELAND:
Marc Prochasson
A Voluntary Association of Returned Development Workers for the Promotion
   of International Development Cooperation (Comhlamh)
61 Lower Camden Street
2 Dublin
Tel: +35/31-783490
Fax: +35/31-783738

ITALY:
Gioia Maestro
National Association of Italian Communities (ANCI)
Piazza Duomo 21
20121 Milano
Tel: +39/2-72004079
Fax: +39/2-68009266

Ana Foca
Molisv
Piazza Albania 10
00153 Rome
Tel: +39/6-5750941
Fax: +39/6-5744869

JAPAN:
Shin Yoshida
Community Link International
Kita-ku, Tabata 1-21-18
114 Tokyo
Tel: +81/3-56851177
Fax: +81/3-56850550

Kiyoshi Matsuya
Association of Local Legislators for a Better Environment
169-4 Johoku
Shizuoka City
Tel: +81/54-2510035
Fax: +81/54-2515021

LITHUANIA:
Virginia Sestakauskiene
Association of Lithuanian Cities
P.O. Box 251
3000 Kaunas-C
Tel: +370/2-221471
Fax: +370/2-618689

THE NETHERLANDS:
Paul van Tongeren
National Commission for Development Education (NCO)
P.O. Box 18184
1001 ZB Amsterdam
Tel: +31/20-5503555
Fax: +31/20-6208716

Wico Bunskoek
Conference Centre "Kontakt der Kontinenten"
Amersfoortseweg 20
3769 AS Soesterberg
Tel: +31/3463-51755
Fax: +31/3463-54735

Peter Knip
Association of Netherlands Municipalities
P.O. Box 30435
2500 GK The Hague
Tel: +31/70-3738393
Fax: +31/70-3635682

Dion van den Berg
Interchurch Peace Council (IKV)
Celebesstraat 60
2508 CN The Hague
Tel: +31/70-3507100
Fax: +31/70-3542611

Ronald van der Hijden
National Council for City Linking Netherlands-Nicaragua
P.O. Box 202
1000 AE Amsterdam
Tel: +31/20-5522505
Fax: +31/20-5523426

Hans Buis
Platform South Africa
Association of Netherlands Municipalities
P.O. Box 30435
2500 GK The Hague
Tel: +31/70-3738675
Fax: +31/70-3635682

NORWAY:
Tor Henrik Anderson
Friendship North South
P.O. Box 220
Sentrum
N-10103 Oslo
Tel: +47/2-333053
Fax: +47/2-333051

PORTUGAL:
North–South Centre
Av. da Liberdade 229-6
1200 Lisbon
Tel: +351/1-522903
Fax: +351/1-531329

Mr. Jardim
Oikos
Av. Visconde Valmor 35-3 Dto
Lisbon
Tel: +351/1-7964719
Fax: +351/1-7939791

SPAIN:
Hans Devos
Institute for Study and Documentation of Africa and Latin America
Calle Hermanos G. Noblejas 4
28037 Madrid
Tel: +34/1-4084112
Fax: +34/1-4087047

Luz Romano
Federation of Spanish Municipalities and Provences (FEMP)
Calle Nuncio 8
28005 Madrid
Tel: +34/1-2659406
Fax: +34/1-2655482

Nuria Camps i Vidal
Fondo Catalan
Rivadeneyra no. 6-1DE
08002 Barcelona
Tel: +34/3-4122602
Fax: +34/3-4125384

SWITZERLAND:
Jean Pierre Gontard
Federation Genevoise de Cooperation
10 Rue Richemont
1202 Geneve
Tel: +41/22-7380488
Fax: +41/22-7385959

Gabrielle Nanchen
Cooperation Suisse au Developement Questions Nord Sud
CH-1977 Icogne
Tel: +41/27-432292

UK:
Paul Bongers
Local Government International Bureau
35 Great Smith Street
SW1P 3BJ London
Tel: +44/71-2221636
Fax: +44/71-2332179

Mary Stead
United Kingdom One World Linking Association (UKOWLA)
Chesterfield Borough Council
Townhall
Chesterfield S40 1LP
Tel: +44/865-791610

Jane Knight
International Liaison Officer, Towns and Development
1 Barrowfield Lane
Kenilworth
CV8 1EP
Tel/Fax: +44/926-864243

USA:
Michael Shuman
Institute for Policy Studies (IPS)
1601 Connecticut Ave., NW
Washington, DC 20009
Tel: +1/202-234-9382
Fax: +1/202-387-7915

John Donaldson
Sister Cities International
120 South Payne Street
Alexandria, Virginia 22314
Tel: +1/703-8363535
Fax: +1/703-8364815

Contacts in the South

ARGENTINA:
Maria Onestini (T&D regional coordinator - Latin America)
Centre of Environmental Studies
Avenida Cordoba 1539
1c, 1055 Buenos Aires
C. Correo 116 - suc 28 (1428)
Buenos Aires
Tel: +54/1-8126490
Fax: +54/1-8126490 or +54/1-3130132

COSTA RICA:
Huberth Mendez
Municipality of San Jose
Apartado 5102-1000
San Jose
Tel: +506/552850
Fax: +506/223210

INDIA:
Manohar Golpelwar (T&D regional coordinator - Asia)
Indian Institute of Youth Welfare
134 Shivaji Nagar
Nagpur 440010
Tel: +91/712-533421
Fax: +91/712-524163

KENYA:
Salim Mungai
Kenya Adult Education Association
P.O. Box 22070
Nairobi
Tel: +254/2-221451
Fax: +254/2-340849

MEXICO:
Luis Nava
Equipo Pueblo
Privada M. Otero 255
San Luis Potosi
Tel: +52/48-133236
Fax: +52/48-126289

NICARAGUA:
Monica Baltodano
Popol Na
Apartado 4611
Managua
Tel: +505/2-666628
Fax: +505/2-660133

PHILIPPINES:
Horacio Morales
Philippines Rural Reconstruction Movement
940 Cemzon Avenue
Quezon City
Tel: +63/2-991715
Fax: +63/2-997919

ZIMBABWE:
Michael Ndubiwa
City of Bulawayo
P.O. Box 591
Tel: +263/9-65657
Fax: +263/9-79304

Peter Nyoni (T&D regional coordinator - Africa)
Africa Community-based Development Initiatives
P.O. Box 1818
Tel/Fax: +263/9-72127
Telex.   33463 ZW

International Contacts

Peter Slits
International Union of Local Authorities
Wassenaarseweg 39
2509 LP The Hague
The Netherlands
Tel: +31/70-3244032
Fax: +31/70-3246916

Ron Kingham
Environment and Development Centre
Boulevard Brand Whitlock 146
1200 Brussels
Belgium
Tel: +32/2-7368050
Fax: +32/2-733-5708

Jaap Huurman
Nultimational (Triangular Linking)
Schalkburgerstraat 427
2572 TC The Hague
The Netherlands
Tel: +31/70-3892825

Jeb Brugmann
International Council for Local Environmental Initiatives (ICLEI)
City Hall East Tower 8th Floor
Toronto, Ontario M5H 2N2
Canada
Tel: +1/416-3921462
Fax: +1/416-3921478

Otto Zimmerman
ICLEI Europe
Eschholzstr. 86
D-79115 Freiburg
Germany
Tel: +49/761-368920
Fax: +49/761-368260

Annotated Bibliography

The best information about community-based development initiatives is available from Towns and Development (PO Box 85615, 2508 CH The Hague, Netherlands). For almost a decade Towns and Development has been producing booklets, conference reports, and newsletters that document the evolution of CDIs in various parts of the world.

In preparation for a conference in Berlin in October 1992, Towns and Development commissioned 38 reports on CDIs that provided the factual input for this book, all of which are available from its main office in the Hague. Another useful document produced for the Berlin conference is a compendium of 49 CDI case studies from Austria, Belgium, Canada, Germany, Japan, the Netherlands, Norway, Switzerland, the United Kingdom, and the United States.

The first major study Towns and Development prepared was for the Cologne conference of 1985. Entitled *NGO and Local Authority Joint Action for North–South Cooperation* and written by Nico Kussendrager, it described examples of CDIs in Belgium, Germany, the Netherlands, and the United Kingdom. This report, updated in 1988, remains an excellent introduction to the field, filled with user-friendly pictures, testimonials, quotes, and graphics.

In subsequent years Towns and Development sponsored seminars in which participants submitted papers that were later published in bound volumes. Vernon Smith edited a booklet in 1987 called "From Local to Global: Working with Local Authorities on International Issues." A 1988 compendium, based on a conference in Bremen, was on "Strategies and Future Perspectives." A 1990 report on "Linking/Twinning and Project Support: A Means for Development Education and Awareness Raising?" contained input papers from the European Community, Flanders, the Netherlands, Norway, Scotland, and the United Kingdom.

In 1992 Peter Batty of the United Kingdom prepared a grassroots manual on CDIs for Towns and Development entitled *Global Issues: A Local Challenge*. Aimed primarily at activists in the North, the handbook explains why development cooperation should be a priority for Northern localities and how, step by step, communities can create successful linkages with the South. The manual is written in a punchy, question-and-answer style. A pamphlet-length version is also available.

Towns and Development has produced several interesting video tapes, including half-hour documentaries about the CDI conferences in Bulawayo, Zimbabwe, and Sevagram, India. Another film, *From Cologne to Berlin*, was prepared for the Berlin conference and focuses on a dozen of the most successful CDIs throughout the world.

One can get a good flavor of CDIs from the newsletters of the leading international organizations of municipalities, such as the International Union of Local Authorities (IULA) in the Hague and the United Towns Organisation (UTO) in Paris. Periodic reports are available from international organizations promoting various issue networks, including the International Council for Local Environmental Initiatives (Toronto and Freiburg) and the International Nuclear Free Zone Registry (Manchester).

In almost every country with CDIs, leading NGOs have produced handbooks and newsletters on linking, twinning, development education, campaigning, alternative trade, and other initiatives. Interested readers should contact the organizations listed in Appendix III. A summary of the resources available from these groups, most of which are not in English, can be found in Peter Batty's manual, *Global Issues: A Local Challenge*.

The universe of English materials is smaller but still impressive:

Canada. In 1991 the Federation of Canadian Municipalities' (FCM) International Program issued a report on "Success Stories" concerning its town-twinning program. It also has published several interesting papers, including "Aid and Trade: New Municipal Roles in International Development" (June 1987), "A Practical Guide to Municipal Twinning" (May 1988), and "Meeting the Challenge: Urban Development in the Third World" (June 1989). Indicative of Canada's special efforts at promoting technical assistance, FCM has produced pamphlets and papers on its Africa 2000 and other programs linking Canadian and Southern civil servants.

Germany. The city-state of Bremen has an English compendium of documents on its Development Cooperation Program, and the father of the program, Gunther Hilliges, regularly writes English-language papers on the involvement of German cities in North–South development cooperation. English versions of various declarations of the North–South Campaign in Germany are also available, including those from Mainz (1988), Bonn (1990), and Berlin (1991).

Greece. The Hellenic Institute of Cooperation and Solidarity with Developing Countries periodically publishes an English-language version of its magazine *Synergasia: Cooperation North–South.*

The Netherlands. Paul van Tongeren of NCO has been a prolific observer and analyst of CDIs, producing a steady stream of papers and reports on the subject. His monographs include "International Aspects of Municipal Policy" (1989) and "Think Globally, Act Locally: Town Twinning As A New Vehicle for North–South Cooperation" (1990, co-written by Wim Hart). The Association of Netherland Municipalities (VNG) has published three interesting publications: "VNG and Municipal International Cooperation," "The Netherlands Inter-municipal Development Cooperation Programme," and "Netherlands Municipalities and Development Cooperation." In 1991 the city of Amsterdam produced an attractive pamphlet on its "Development Cooperation Policy." Many Dutch NGOs that have pioneered CDIs produce English-language reports of their work; these include Friends of the Earth (tropical timber campaign), the Europe–Nicaragua Network, the Max Havelaar Foundation (solidarity coffee campaign), Platform South Africa (anti-apartheid campaigns), and IKV (peace and anti-nuclear-weapon campaigns).

Nicaragua. The Popol Na Foundation for the Promotion of Municipal Development recently completed an impressive study on "Local Development Projects: The Town Twinning Movement in Nicaragua (1980-90)."

United Kingdom. The two main sources of information about CDIs in the United Kingdom are Jane Knight, formerly with Oxfam-UK and now a staff member of Towns and Development, and the United Kingdom One World Linking Association (UKOWLA). In 1990 UKOWLA commissioned Peter Batty to prepare a "Community Link Handbook." The Local Government International Bureau periodically publishes booklets and pamphlets on CDIs, including "Safari," in which authors Peter Batty and Musa Njiru explain how groups can prepare themselves for North–South exchanges and visits. Two other interesting handbooks have been recently produced in the United Kingdom. One is *You, Gloucestershire, the World, & You: A Handbook on Organising Local Action for Global Change,* written by Martin Simon and Melanie Gummer. The other is Rex Beddis' and Cherry Marris' *School Links International: A New Approach to Primary School Linking Around the World.*

United States. Each of the two principal networks in the United States has its special resources. The traditional network is overseen by Sister Cities International, which publishes a magazine and several reports each year. The more political CDIs are documented in the *Bulletin of Municipal Foreign Policy* (1986–91) and *Global Communities* (1991–93), both available from the Institute for Policy Studies. A superb book describing grassroots North–South initiatives is Medea Benjamin's and Andrea Freedman's *Bridging the Global Gap: A Handbook to Linking Citizens of the First and Third Worlds* (Cabin John, MD: Seven Locks, 1990).

Index